1919–21 A GLOBAL HISTORY

EDITORIAL

EDITORS
Tommy Graham and Brian Hanley

COMMISSIONING EDITORS
Fearghal McGarry and Enda Delaney

EDITORIAL BOARD
Tony Canavan
Elma Collins
Peter Collins
Patrick Fitzgerald
Brian Hanley
Angus Mitchell
Éamonn Ó Ciardha
Eamon O'Flaherty
Thomas O'Loughlin

PUBLISHING MANAGER
Nick Maxwell

DESIGN
Ger Garland

COPY-EDITING
Emer Condit

PRINTED IN IRELAND BY
W&G Baird Ltd.

A *History Ireland* annual
FIRST PUBLISHED BY HISTORY
PUBLICATIONS LTD 2019,
Unit 9, 78 Furze Road, Sandyford
Industrial Estate, Dublin 18.
T. (+ 353 1) 2933568
F. (+ 353 1) 2939377
W. www.historyireland.com

ISBN 978-0-9935328-2-5
First published 2019

British Library Cataloguing-in-Publication
Data. A catalogue record for this book is
available from the British Library.

Preface

Welcome to *The Irish Revolution 1919–21*
History Ireland's stand-alone supplements tra
Centenaries'. Given the success of the last two ̶ ̶ ̶ ̶ ̶ ̶ ̶ ̶ ̶ ̶ ̶ ̶ ̶ ̶ ̶
1916–18: changed utterly—we are confident that this latest offering will prove
equally popular with our readers.

Nevertheless, at the outset it presented certain challenges. Since the
ground-breaking *Politics and Irish life, 1913–1921: provincial experience of war
and revolution* (1977) by David Fitzpatrick (sadly no longer with us), the local
study (in this case of County Clare) has been the dominant approach to our
understanding of the Irish Revolution. In the intervening years a proliferation of equally scholarly local studies have appeared (and with more to
come), culminating in Cork University Press's excellent *Atlas of the Irish
Revolution*, also the basis for RTÉ's three-part documentary *The Irish
Revolution* (to be reviewed in the July/August 2019 issue of the magazine).
How could we do justice to the sheer quantity of such material in a 100-page
publication such as this? And in any case would we simply be reinventing
the wheel?

A chance conversation with Fearghal McGarry two years ago provided a
possible answer to my dilemma. Fearghal explained that he was working on
a joint research proposal—between Queen's University Belfast, the University
of Edinburgh and Boston College—for a collaborative research project entitled 'A Global History of Irish Revolution, 1916–1923'. The aim was to
integrate two sophisticated but separate historiographical fields—the Irish
Revolution and Irish migration—to develop a more inclusive framework that
would incorporate the diaspora and other external pressures into the mainstream narrative. To what extent did revolutionary developments outside
Ireland shape what happened within? And in what ways did events within
during the revolutionary period have an impact beyond Irish shores—what
influence did they have, for instance, upon the large Irish diaspora population and amongst other national groups?

My interest was further piqued when Fearghal explained that, as well as
the usual resulting academic publications, workshops and an international
conference (to be held in Boston College in spring 2020), the project was
keen to publicise its findings amongst the wider history-reading public as
soon as possible. A job for *History Ireland*, surely? I needed no second invitation: memos were exchanged, a contract was drawn up and the result is the
present collection of articles. We hope you find them stimulating.

***

I'm grateful to Fearghal and to Enda Delaney not only for commissioning
the articles but also for ensuring that the various contributors delivered user-
friendly copy (and on time!). They in turn would like to acknowledge the
support of the UK's Arts and Humanities Research Council. A particular word
of thanks is due to Brian Hanley, without whose last-minute heroic efforts
this publication would not have gotten across the line. As usual, for the pro-
vision of images we are indebted to our efficient but sometimes hard-pressed
national institutions—the National Library of Ireland, the National Museum
of Ireland, Kilmainham Gaol, UCD Archives, Dublin City Library and
Archive and the Military Archives—as well as overseas institutions such as
the National Archives UK, the National Portrait Gallery, London, and the US
Library of Congress. Every effort has been made to obtain permission for the
reproduction of images that may be subject to copyright; if we have erred in
that regard, please get in touch and we will rectify in later editions.

Tommy Graham

HISTORY IRELAND

...many soldiers went straight fro the battlefields of the Great War policing the Empire.

79

Irish-American women protest in Washington DC, 1920—women played a major role in the agitation that developed in the United States during the War of Independence.

51

The Irish leader proved an enduring inspiration for colonial peoples.

84

BOND DRIVE, an ambitious fund-raising campaign that targeted the Irish diaspora in the United States.

37

41 Making the case for an Irish republic entailed extensive social engagement.

1919–21 A GLOBAL HISTORY

HISTORY IRELAND

www.historyireland.com

A GLOBAL HISTORY OF IRISH REVOLUTION   BY **ENDA DELANEY**

When we think of the course of Ireland's revolution, we inevitably start with the First World War and the Easter Rising of 1916, critical events that, in very different ways, placed the Irish experience firmly on the global stage. The end of the war in 1918 set in train a series of initiatives in international diplomacy that Irish republicans sought to harness for their own ends, most obviously the Wilsonian doctrine and the Paris Peace Conference of 1919.

Self-determination and the rights of small nations, the compelling doctrines of the new post-war world order, had much to offer Irish nationalists. The post-war world presented opportunities and potential models for Irish republicans seeking to bring an end to British rule in Ireland. In large part, the effort to globalise the Irish revolution, masterminded by one of the most outward-looking European nationalist movements, concentrated on communicating with both Irish and non-Irish audiences.

Populations of Irish descent across the world were mobilised in the United States, Canada, Britain, Australia, New Zealand, South Africa and Argentina, to help spread the revolutionary message and to support the campaign for independence at home and abroad. The fledgling Irish diplomatic service played an important role in connecting the Irish cause to people outside Ireland, whether they were Irish or not.

Press coverage of the revolution was crucial in drawing attention to events in Ireland, especially the British campaign to counter both the activities of the Dáil government and the guerrilla war waged against Crown forces by the IRA. Dramatic episodes such as Terence MacSwiney's hunger strike gripped not only Irish but also global attention. Prominent Irish leaders such as Éamon de Valera and Hanna Sheehy Skeffington made important visits to the United States, and across the 'Irish world', which received extensive coverage.

What is often neglected in Irish accounts of this story is that what was happening at home was both a source of inspiration for anti-colonialists across the world and a practical manifestation of the limitations of an imperial power's ability to suppress a revolutionary democratic impulse through a controversial campaign of political and military repression.

Standing back from forensic investigation of events in Ireland between 1916 and 1923 to consider how we present a global history of Irish revolution brings into sharp focus themes that rarely feature in our consciousness. Race, for instance, was a vital element of Irish revolutionary encounters with other ethnic groups across the world. Irish radicals had contacts with many different peoples in many diverse places. And anti-colonialism had dimensions that stretched far beyond the island of Ireland to Egypt, India, Africa and Spanish America. Nor did Irish republicans always face easy decisions in calculating how best to exploit these international opportunities. Opening up a line of communication with Bolsheviks in Russia in 1920/21 to seek support for Irish independence was a very risky initiative, given the potential for alienating the Catholic Church.

What does a global history offer that we do not already have in many accomplished histories of Irish revolution? In the first instance, there is the much-needed perspective afforded by standing back from events in Ireland to understand the wider context of post-war Europe, and equally Ireland's place in the newly reconfigured western world, where empires were now in irreversible decline.

Widening the focus from the history of the Irish overseas to the global significance of the 'Irish question' enables us to chart how extensively the conflict in Ireland was debated across the world in anti-imperial, labour, suffragist, dominion and other circles. Such an approach offers a way of broadening out consideration of the global dimensions of the Irish revolution beyond the involvement of the diaspora in activities such as fund-raising. Nevertheless, there is no doubt that the effort to raise funds from the global Irish diaspora was crucial in financing the Irish revolution.

What also emerges clearly is how transnational communications, primarily newspapers and the telegraph, fundamentally shaped how the Irish revolution was reported and written about. The digitisation of newspapers now allows for this story to be told from many different places.

Finally, and most importantly, the growth in digital archives such as the 1911 Irish Census of Population, the Bureau of Military History and the Military Service Pensions Collection enables people, wherever they happen to be located in the world, to explore in unprecedented detail the fascinating and rich history of Ireland's global revolution.

Enda Delaney is Professor of Modern History at the University of Edinburgh, and co-principal investigator of the UK Arts and Humanities Research Council-funded project A Global History of Irish Revolution, 1916–1923.

> *'Ireland to-day reasserts her historic nationhood the more confidently before the new world emerging from the War, because she believes in freedom and justice as the fundamental principles of international law.'*
>
> —'Message to the Free Nations of the World', 21 January 1919

SETTING THE SCENE

We claim for our national independence the recognition and support of every free nation in the world, and we proclaim that independence to be a condition precedent to international peace hereafter.

—Dáil Éireann, Declaration of Independence, 21 January 1919

Image: 'IRELAND'S APPEAL TO EUROPE … rendered into verse of easy flowing metre, it [...] should strike a responsive echo in the hearts of all true lovers of liberty, ultimately forcing Civilization to insist upon the recognition of our demands on a footing with those of Serbia, Belgium, and Poland.'

REFRAMING IRELAND'S REVOLUTION

BY **FEARGHAL McGARRY**

How should we interpret the conflicts over sovereignty that occurred in Ireland between 1916 and 1923? As a distinctively Irish phenomenon, largely determined by events on the island, or as a product of global forces unleashed by the Great War that saw multinational empires give way to nation-states across much of Europe? Which frameworks—local, national, transnational or global—are most useful for analysing the violent process of state formation in Ireland?

A notable historiographical shift in recent decades is acceptance of the idea that the Easter Rising 'can

only be properly understood in the context of the Great War'. As Keith Jeffery argued in *1916: a global history*, 'As surely as Verdun or the Somme, Dublin in 1916 was a First World War battlefield'. In contrast, there is less public awareness of the extent to which the War of Independence was similarly shaped by external forces. As Maurice Walsh notes in *Bitter freedom*, the conflict is too often narrated 'in a claustrophobic Anglo-Irish setting, with the global war a mere backdrop to the drama in Ireland'.

Commemoration of the revolutionary period provides one example. By incorporating remembrance of the First World War and Easter 1916

within a 'Decade of Centenaries', the Irish state ensured that both conflicts, previously understood as parallel events, were increasingly seen to form, in Jeffery's words, 'a seamless robe' of Irish experience. In contrast, the time-line of significant historical events proposed by the Irish state's Expert Advisory Group for Commemorations to mark 'The Independence Struggle 1919–1921'— beginning with the convening of the Dáil in January 1919 and ending with the burning of the Custom House in May 1921—lists only events that occurred within Ireland (or the UK).

Although historians understand how external pressures shaped Ireland's revolution, our tendency to write narratives centring on what Irish people did in Ireland to win independence makes it difficult to assess the significance of these wider forces. Nation-state frameworks allow for a coherent narrative, one that the public likes to read, in which Irish people take centre stage, achieving, through their own agency, their liberation after decades or centuries of struggle. The county study, the dominant approach since David Fitzpatrick's ground-breaking *Politics and Irish life, 1913–1921: provincial experience of war and revolution* (1977), has reinforced this tendency to confine studies of the revolution within the island. Local studies offer a rich template for anatomising processes of revolutionary change, such as political mobilisation or levels of violence, but are less effective in terms of analysing causal factors, particularly those resulting from external pressures. Why, for example, did nationalist expectations change so radically between 1914, when Home Rule was widely seen as an acceptable settlement, to 1918, when the Irish Republic won broad electoral support? The principal reason is that the world beyond Ireland was rapidly and fundamentally transformed by developments such as the publication of President Wilson's Fourteen Points and the Paris Peace Conference.

While the most innovative micro-studies—such as Peter Hart's research on sectarian violence in Cork—use a small scale to investigate

large problems, county studies often demonstrate less ambitious objectives. Some seek merely to address a neglected region or, as with one recent publication, to demonstrate how a 'slack' county was, in fact, 'at the forefront of the struggle for Irish freedom'. Historians such as Colin Reid have argued that the significance of political ideas such as self-determination and unionism have been neglected by many studies of the revolution. One reason may be the preoccupation of local studies with counting that which can be measured—votes, strikes, branches of organisations or shootings. 'However skilful and illuminating in themselves', the late David Fitzpatrick has recently observed, the proliferation of localised studies has 'yielded no general pattern beyond the infinite variety of revolutionary activity' and the 'importance of local peculiarities'.

Studies framed within the nation-state (whether defined as Ireland or the UK) pose similar challenges. Charles Townshend's *The British campaign in Ireland* (1975) brilliantly analyses Britain's counter-insurrectionary campaign in Ireland, but with little reference to the wider imperial factors that influenced it. One reason, for example, why Churchill made the fateful decision to form the 'Black-and-Tans' was the cabinet's concerns about the military resources required to suppress unrest in India and Egypt. Wider imperial considerations were central to many aspects of the Irish conflict, including the British government's unwillingness to offer substantial political sovereignty to republicans until 1921 and the revolution's ultimately unsatisfactory outcome for republicans.

Understanding how the global shapes the national is not a new challenge. The discipline of history, Richard White observed, is 'a child of the nation-state': since 'the nation-state became the stage, historians have almost automatically used it as the preferred scale for their work'. Indeed, given the importance of the Irish diaspora, historians of Ireland are probably less insular than their peers. At a recent conference on the impact of the First World War on the

United Kingdom's home front, I was struck by how little Ireland, then part of the UK, featured in many contributions. A keynote speaker disputed the idea that a revolutionary threat (emanating from the Red Clydeside) to the UK existed in 1919. It took an intervention from the floor, from an Irish historian, to point out that a revolution actually occurred in the post-war UK, one resulting in territorial changes similar to those experienced by the defeated Central Powers. The proposition that the UK (as opposed to Great Britain) largely escaped the post-war pressures that assailed other European empires suggests a retrospective imposition of geographical—and mental—borders that did not exist at the time. Contemporary intelligence records, in contrast, indicate that

reactionary officials such as Sir Henry Wilson had, if anything, an exaggerated perception of the interconnectedness of anti-colonial uprisings, Soviet subversion, labour agitation in Britain and the 'Irish question'.

In *The Wilsonian moment* (2007), the first major study of 1919 from a non-European perspective, Erez Manela argues that much of what historical actors saw and did at this time is rendered incomprehensible, even invisible, without an awareness

Above: The Friends of Irish Freedom publicise the results of the 1918 general election in the United States. (NLI)

Opposite page: Marcus Garvey speaks at Harlem's Liberty Hall—the black nationalist leader saw the Irish cause as central to the struggle for African freedom.

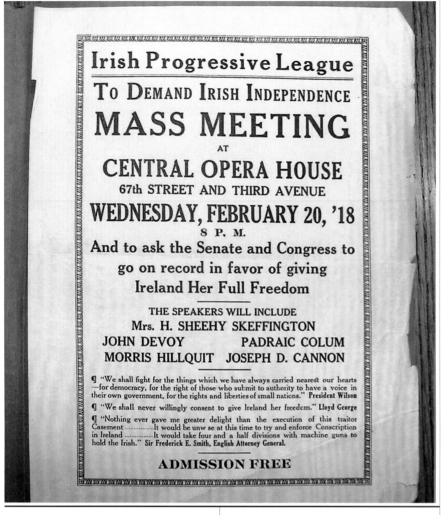

Irish Progressive League
To Demand Irish Independence
MASS MEETING
AT
CENTRAL OPERA HOUSE
67th STREET AND THIRD AVENUE
WEDNESDAY, FEBRUARY 20, '18
8 P. M.
And to ask the Senate and Congress to
go on record in favor of giving
Ireland Her Full Freedom

THE SPEAKERS WILL INCLUDE
Mrs. H. SHEEHY SKEFFINGTON
JOHN DEVOY   PADRAIC COLUM
MORRIS HILLQUIT   JOSEPH D. CANNON

¶ "We shall fight for the things which we have always carried nearest our hearts—for democracy, for the right of those who submit to authority to have a voice in their own government, for the rights and liberties of small nations." President Wilson
¶ "We shall never willingly consent to give Ireland her freedom." Lloyd George
¶ "Nothing ever gave me greater delight than the execution of this traitor Casement ....It would be unwise at this time to try and enforce Conscription in Ireland ....It would take four and a half divisions with machine guns to hold the Irish." Sir Frederick E. Smith, English Attorney General.

ADMISSION FREE

studies of nationalism are generally rooted within national frameworks. Major histories of Irish nationalism, such as Richard English's formidable *Irish freedom* (subtitled 'The history of nationalism *in* Ireland'), acknowledge but do not analyse the impact of the diaspora on Irish nationalism. Although noting 'the enormous impact of long-distance nationalism on the course of nationalism back in Ireland', Brundage's important study of diasporic nationalism remains 'a history of Irish nationalists *in* the United States'. By bringing connections between both of these spheres into clearer focus, placing the revolution in its global context will offer new perspectives on old questions.

How might it be done? One approach is to reverse the nation-state bias by prioritising investigation of how interactions *across* national boundaries shaped Ireland's revolution. For example, how did external influences shape the revolution *within* Ireland? And what impact did the revolution in Ireland have on Irish nationalism, and other peoples and movements, *beyond* the island? A key idea underlying such transnational approaches—that historical processes are not merely 'made in different places but constructed in the movement between places, sites and regions'—is demonstrated by many of the essays in this publication.

Consideration of the global will allow for comparative insights. Although Erez Manela's study, *The Wilsonian moment*, assesses how nationalist hopes in Egypt, India, China and Korea were raised—and dashed—by Wilson's advocacy of self-determination, his findings are applicable to Ireland's revolution. Self-determination, Manela demonstrates, supplied a language of revolution that underpinned anti-colonial challenges to the old order. The belief that their cause could be placed before the international community further undermined imperial legitimacy, encouraging nationalists to reject offers of limited reform in favour of full independence. Imperial intransigence in the face of these demands in turn fuelled resistance, broadening the social base of

of the wider international context. David Lloyd has noted parallels between the fragmentation of territory relied on by colonial powers and the way in which national boundaries are retrospectively imposed by scholarly disciplines. Situating research within a national or local context makes it more difficult to assess this wider international context, particu-

Above: 'Come in your thousands and prove that the Irish are for Freedom everywhere'—the left-wing Irish Progressive League support socialist Morris Hillquit for mayor of New York in October 1917. (NLI)

Opposite page, above: 'RUSSIA RECOGNISES IRELAND. IRELAND! RESPOND TO RUSSIA!'—a cross-section of Irish republican and labour figures speak at a rally in the Mansion House, Dublin, in support of the Bolsheviks in February 1918. (NLI)

Opposite page, below: Indian nationalist Lala Lajpat Rai, a close collaborator with Irish activists in the United States.

larly the extent to which the destabilising impact of the First World War, the post-war acceptance of national self-determination as the principal source of political legitimacy and the emergence of twenty new republics across Europe heightened political expectations in Ireland. Even the imperialist *Irish Times*, reflecting on the likely legacy of the Great War in December 1918, appeared to acknowledge that the game was up: 'America not England will be the interpreter of the thoughts and visions of the world re-born'.

Enda Delaney has noted how, on leaving Ireland, emigrants become the preserve of a separate sphere, diasporic history, resulting in a disconnection between our understanding of the experiences of the Irish at home and abroad. Similarly, although modern nationalism is an international phenomenon, forged by transnational ideas and forces, nationalist movements and reinforcing their commitment to goals that were viewed as unrealistic before the First World War. As in Ireland, this was a long process: Britain granted Egypt limited independence in 1922 (the same year the Irish Free State was established); Egypt won greater independence in 1936 (a year before Ireland did so), and full separation in 1956 (seven years after the establishment of an Irish republic). In both countries, the political impact of this formative post-war moment was enduring: the party created to place Egyptian claims before the Paris Conference dominated Egypt for three decades; in the Irish Republic, the parties created by the Treaty split are still dominant, while Northern Irish politics remain structured around the legacy of partition.

Manela's study also highlights how anti-colonial activists shared a revolutionary methodology. Mass movements at home and expatriate networks abroad were mobilised in support of national self-determination. An outpouring of pamphlets and declarations drew on Wilsonian language to articulate long-standing grievances, while the importance of claiming a place on the international stage provided vital leverage for popular mobilisation at home. Much of this revolutionary activism took the form of interactions across territorial boundaries, particularly within the 'contact zones' of anti-imperial metropolises such as Paris, New York and London. Focusing on events

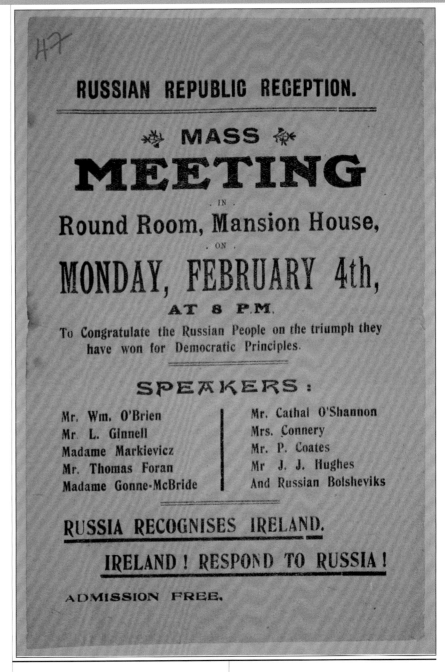

within Ireland can overstate the novelty of Sinn Féin's approach when considered within this wider context. As Maurice Walsh noted, 'As the Hapsburg, Ottoman and Russian Empires crumbled, other subject nationalities threw up their own Redmonds and de Valeras debating the merits of co-operation or resistance', and it was not only in Ireland that the resisters 'were in the ascendant' by 1918.

Recognition of these broader patterns raises questions about causality. Histories of the War of Independence place republican agency at the centre of their frameworks. Given that the strength of the republican challenge was largely a consequence of the weakening of imperial power, however, causality might be more usefully considered from the 'outside in'. The catalysts for revolution in Ireland, such as the Easter Rising and the conscription crisis, stemmed directly from the First World War. Sinn Féin's success in 1918 formed part of the post-war high tide of national self-determination movements across Europe and beyond. Partition, and the emergence of two Irish states, formed part of

Above: Crowds outside the Mansion House, Dublin, await news of the truce negotiations in July 1921. The Stars and Stripes illustrate a continuing attachment to the belief that America would come to Ireland's aid. (NMI)

the post-war redrawing of boundaries that saw majoritarian nation-states proliferate across Europe.

The comparative also allows for consideration of differences: in contrast to the new republics that emerged from the vacuum left by the collapse of the Continental empires, Irish nationalists sought to carve out a republic at the periphery of a victorious—if weakened—empire. British state power ensured that Ireland's revolution was a managed process, limiting violence but, as with Manela's anti-colonial movements, frustrating aspirations for full independence.

Consideration of these wider patterns raises questions about the timing of challenges to empire (which historians tend to analyse over long periods of time): events in Ireland in 1918 and early 1919, such as the conscription crisis, the general election and the establishment of the Dáil, remain relatively neglected in comparison to the much smaller mobilisation of 1916, widely seen as the Irish revolution's year zero. A wider context will also help to illuminate changing patterns of violence. The violence of the War of Independence, the conflict in Ulster and the Irish Civil War echoed wider patterns of revolutionary violence that swept Central and Eastern Europe between 1918 and 1923, where imperial power was challenged by democratisation, self-determination and ethnic nationalism. In these regions, conflict between state forces gave way, after 1918, to paramilitary and ethno-sectarian violence that blurred the distinction between combatants and civilians and generated new forms of political authority.

Comparisons can also help in considering differences of scale. If Finland, a country with a similar population to Ireland, experienced twenty times more violence in its contemporaneous civil war, should we think more about the violence that did *not* happen than about the exceptional atrocities that occupy so much of our attention? Tim Wilson's comparative analysis of violence in Ulster and Silesia, for example, may tell us more about Irish violence than ever-more-detailed micro-studies of killings in West Cork.

Finally, 'decentring' Irish nationalism will provide new perspectives on Irish nationalist politics. Beyond the nation, what it meant to be Irish was shaped by contingency, with political and social attitudes reflecting the environments in which the Irish found themselves. That Irish nationalism could mean different things in different places, more bound up with labour politics in the US or Australia in contrast to a more socially conservative movement at home, raises questions about the formation of Irish identity. Similarly, attitudes to topics such as race, which varied considerably across the 'Irish world', will lend themselves more readily to consideration on a wider canvas. Ultimately, as this supplement aims to demonstrate, a global perspective will help us to understand how Ireland's revolution formed part of a wider ideological moment in world history.

Fearghal McGarry is Professor of Modern Irish History at Queen's University Belfast and principal investigator of the UK Arts and Humanities Research Council-funded project A Global History of Irish Revolution, 1916–1923.

THE POST-WAR ORDER

The more I think of the President's declaration as to the right of 'self-determination' the more convinced I am of the danger of putting such ideas into the minds of certain races ... What effect will it have on the Irish, the Indians, the Egyptians, and the nationalists among the Boers? ... The phrase is simply loaded with dynamite. It will raise hopes which can never be realised.

—Robert Lansing, US secretary of state,
The peace negotiations: a personal narrative (1921)

Image: *The Signing of Peace in the Hall of Mirrors, Versailles, 28 June 1919* by William Orpen. (IWM)

MAKING THE NEW EUROPE: THE POST-WAR POLITICAL ORDER

BY **WILLIAM MULLIGAN**

The New Europe, published in 1918, was Thomas Masaryk's programmatic statement of principles underlying his aims for the post-war political order. The Czech nationalist, exiled during the First World War, argued that the coming era would be defined by 'the New Man, *Homo Europeus*', an avowed adherent of the nationality principle, democracy and internationalism. Despite this, Masaryk gave short shrift to the claims of Irish nationalists. 'The Irish question,' he claimed, 'is not a national question (not in the sense in which, for example, the Polish or Czechoslovak questions are national questions.' He did not elaborate, but his readiness to identify the Danish claims to Schleswig and Holstein and French claims to Alsace and Lorraine as the only national issues in western Europe highlighted one distinctive dimension of the Irish question: Irish nationalists staked their claims against a victorious Allied power, Britain. Other nation-states in central and eastern Europe emerged from the ruins of four empires—the Russian, Habsburg,

Ottoman and German empires.

Irish nationalists had paid close attention since 1912 to the construction of small nation-states, first in the Balkan Wars of 1912–13, then in the First World War and then in the wars after the war. The period between the onset of the Home Rule crisis in the United Kingdom and the Balkan Wars and the ending of the Civil War in Ireland and the Treaty of Lausanne, the population exchanges between Greece and Turkey, and the stabilisation of states by 1923 saw a reordering of European politics, moving away from imperial and great power politics towards the principle of nationality. Although violated in numerous ways, the nationality principle became the departure point for considerations of the partition of territorial claims and the domestic politics of states. This process proved to be much more violent and less dem-

ocratic in central and eastern Europe than was the case in Ireland. By December 1923 the Hungarian intellectual Oskar Jászi was lamenting that the 'vicious feudal dogma of an absolute national sovereignty makes almost impossible all social life worthy of the name'. Nations, Jászi argued, destroyed the rich transnational networks and cultural exchange that had characterised prewar Europe.

This violent disruption had several sources: the Russian Revolution, ethnic conflict, rival border claims and fraught civil–military relations. These conflicts were interwoven in different ways, so that each local conflict, be it the suppression of the soviet republic in Budapest in 1919 or paramilitary violence in Silesia on the Polish–German border, worked out in distinctive ways. The forms of violence ranged widely, including conven-

tional wars, guerrilla campaigns and assassinations.

By the time of Lenin's death in 1924 the Soviet state had consolidated its power, but the ambitions of the Soviet leadership to promote revolution across the continent and in European imperial possessions had come to naught. Nonetheless, between the Bolshevik seizure of power in November 1917 and the early 1920s, the Russian Revolution injected a radical new dynamic into European politics. Violent revolution spawned an often-vicious counter-revolution, first in Russia and later across Europe. Some of this

●

Opposite page: The 'big four'—Lloyd George (UK), Orlando (Italy), Clemenceau (France) and Woodrow Wilson (USA)—at the peace conference in Paris, 27 May 1919. (Library of Congress)

●

Below: Europe in 1923.

Above: British Prime Minister David Lloyd George signing the Treaty of Versailles on 28 June 1919. (Alamy)

violence was guided directly from Moscow, the new capital of Soviet Russia. After November 1917, the survival of the Bolshevik regime was in doubt. Foreign threats—first from Germany, later from the Allies—combined with the counter-revolutionary White Russian movement to challenge the new Soviet rulers. In the ensuing Russian Civil War an estimated seven million people died; by way of comparison, two million Russian soldiers had died during the First World War and the total death-toll for the First World War, according to Antoine Prost's most recent calculations, is ten million. The Bolshevik leadership adapted and radicalised the techniques of the

Tsarist state for waging war, such as requisitioning food supplies. The formation of the Red Army, with its emphasis on political loyalty and commissars, signalled a new type of conflict, based on an ideologically charged violence between the radical left and counter-revolutionary opponents.

After consolidating power in Russia, Lenin and other Bolshevik leaders sought to export the revolution. Initially their efforts concentrated on former territories of the Russian Empire, notably the Baltics (where they failed, opposed by an unlikely coalition of Baltic nationalists, German paramilitary forces and the Allies) and the Ukraine (which they succeeded in incorporating into the Soviet state). The Polish–Soviet War (1919–21) was the most significant attempt to export revolution.

This war encapsulated the complexity of post-war conflict: from the Polish perspective it was a war of national survival, and it was also part of a triangular conflict between Poland, the Ukrainian nation-state and Russia. Polish forces had invaded the Ukraine in spring 1920 but, overstretched, they found themselves retreating to the edges of Warsaw in the summer of 1920. In Lenin's strategy, the capture of Warsaw promised the best opportunity to export revolution and transform European geopolitics. Lenin was willing to cooperate with Weimar Germany in dismantling the Treaty of Versailles, but he also believed that the Soviet conquest of Poland would prompt communist revolution throughout central Europe, including the fulcrum of European politics, Germany. The battle for Warsaw, Lenin later noted, became a 'turning point for the world'. On 16 August, General Joseph Pilsudski launched a successful counter-attack against the Red Army. Polish workers and farmers rallied to the nation-state, much to the disgust of Bolsheviks such as the Austrian-born Karl Radek, who condemned them for acting 'nationally and imperialistically' rather than 'socially and revolutionarily'. By October 1920 Soviet Russia and Poland had reached a ceasefire, and they signed the Treaty of Riga the following March. Although sporadic attempts to foment revolution continued, defeat at Warsaw marked the effective end of attempts to spread the revolution beyond Russia until the Second World War.

The threatened spread of the Bolshevik revolution radicalised European politics. The Polish government interned 17,000 Jewish men during the war, one of a myriad of examples of the facile but often lethal equation of Jewishness with Bolshevism. The prospect of violent revolution legitimised the formation of local paramilitary groups, such as the *Einwohnerwehr* in Germany and Austria. Paramilitary groups used extreme violence to eradicate the communist threat, often legitimising their actions by claiming to defend national values against Bolshevik internationalism. Short-lived communist republics in Budapest and Munich were suppressed in the spring of 1919. In the White Terror that followed in Munich, paramilitary forces killed an estimated 1,000 people; in Hungary paramilitary groups killed 3,000 people between the fall of the soviet republic in late July 1919 and the end of 1921. Tens of thousands more were packed into jails or fled into exile. In Italy, Mussolini's fascist movement came to prominence by strike-breaking and street violence against left-wing opponents, particularly during the *Biennio Rosso* or Two Red Years of 1919 and 1920. Fascist violence attracted middle-class supporters, who feared the consequences of a left-wing revolution.

The fall of the soviet republic in Budapest was triggered by the invasion of the Romanian army, part of a conflict between Romania and Hungary over Transylvania and another example of the imbrication of revolutionary and national wars. The national conflicts in the region dated back to the nineteenth century, when Greece, Serbia, Romania and Bulgaria had gained their independence but continued to harbour irredentist ambitions. The conflicts intensified during the Balkan Wars (1912–13) and the First World War (1914–18), as each state set about maximising its territorial possessions and nationalising inhabitants. Mass murder and ethnic cleansing accompanied this process, as the forces of the Balkan League killed about 500,000 Muslims and expelled another 500,000 in 1912 and 1913, while the Young Turk regime oversaw the Armenian genocide, in which 1.5 million Armenian Christians died.

Imposing a monochromatic version of the nationality principle on the richly textured ethnic map of eastern and central Europe was a fraught and violent project after 1918. The leaders of new states saw national cohesion not only as an end in itself but also as an essential condition of state security. Foreign states could exploit internal dissent, as Hitler did over the Sudetenland in 1938 to weaken and then destroy the Czechoslovak state. The Versailles settlement included provisions for the protection of minorities, but these were difficult to enforce; moreover, leaders in central and eastern Europe had limited faith that Britain and France would intervene to uphold the territorial integrity of the new states. In short, the demands of nation-making were exacerbated by a security trap, as the new states eyed each other with suspicion and feared the long-term prospect of German and Russian recovery from the war.

Among the most significant conflicts was that between Greece and Turkey. Turkish nationalists forged a new state in Anatolia out of the ruins of the Ottoman Empire.

Atatürk emerged as the key figure in the new state, as he led a campaign against the Greek invasion of Anatolia in 1919 and against the Treaty of Sèvres. The Greek premier, Eleftherios Venizelos, justified the invasion of Anatolia in May 1919 by variously arguing that the local Muslim population would accept Greek rule and that the area had a majority Greek population in any case. Before the Greek forces arrived, Turkish paramilitaries had tried to change facts on the ground by killing and expelling Greek Orthodox civilians. After the Greek forces captured the coastal strip around Smyrna, they too began to alter the local demographic balance, killing and expelling Muslims. Both sides continued to target civilians until the war ended in 1922. The Treaty of Lausanne (1923) included provisions for population exchange, as Muslims were deported to Turkey and Greek Orthodox to Greece. For the individuals deported it was a tragedy. They were uprooted from communities in which they had lived for generations, and national identity was secondary to local identities and religious practices. However, the reasoning behind the population exchange, proposed by the Norwegian humanitarian

●

Below: US Secretary of State Robert Lansing was deeply sceptical about Woodrow Wilson's promises of self-determination.

Fridtjof Nansen, was to limit the scope of future conflict between Greece and Turkey, and in this respect the exchange succeeded. Not until the conflict over Cyprus in the 1950s did the two states clash again.

Civil–military disputes, a prominent feature of European post-war politics with periodic mutinies and military coups, were inter-

● Revolutionaries Rosa Luxemburg (top) and Karl Liebknecht (above), who were murdered after the failure of the Spartacist Rising in Berlin in January 1919.

twined with nationalist rivalries. Take the example of Bulgaria. Disputes over Macedonia plagued relations between Serbia, Greece and Bulgaria from the early twentieth century. Bulgaria had twice ended up on the losing side—in the Second Balkan War (1913) and at the end of the First World War. The post-war prime minister of Bulgaria, Alexander Stamboliski, led BANU, a peasant party committed to land reform at home and peace abroad. Yet his unwillingness to pursue irredentist policies in Macedonia led to conflict with the Bulgarian officer corps and members of the IMRO paramilitary group. The presence of White Russian exiles in Bulgaria only deepened the fault lines of political life. Stamboliski's vision represented an alternative in central and eastern European politics: domestic reform and international cooperation. With large peasant parties in the region, this vision also enjoyed some popularity, but it was not a programme that the influential military could accept. After Stamboliski concluded a treaty with Yugoslavia in February 1923, allowing the Yugoslav army to pursue IMRO paramilitaries over the Bulgarian border, he was a marked man. In June officers launched a coup, murdering Stamboliski, his brother and twenty other BANU deputies. An estimated 16,000 BANU members and communists died in the following two years. Britain and France quickly recognised the new Bulgarian regime, as did Nikolai Pasic, the Serbian prime minister.

The brutal removal of Stamboliski was part of a violent crescendo in post-war European politics in 1923. The Irish Civil War, the French and Belgian occupation of the Ruhr, communist revolts and a Nazi putsch in Germany, and forced relocation of large populations in Greece and Turkey were some of the events that punctuated that year. The stabilisation of European politics seemed distant, but in its own peculiar way the violence paved the way for the restoration of order. That order looked dif-

ferent from the ideals articulated by Wilson in January 1918. Even the poster child of European inter-war democracy, Czechoslovakia, owed its stability to redoubtable administration rather than the accommodation of different interests within a constitutional order.

Judged against the ideals of a Wilson or a Masaryk, the outcome was a bitter mockery of the sacrifices and suffering since 1914. But post-war and post-revolutionary European states generally fall well short of ideals. Indeed, stability may require the compromise of ideals. If one ideal endured, though, it was the nationality principle. Although critics can point to numerous violations of the principle and the existence of large minorities, if we imagine Europe ordered along different principles—economic connections, power politics or confederations of regions, for example—the post-war map would have looked very different. Expecting the full implementation of any principles sets the bar too high for the conduct of politics. Ireland illustrates this point. The border between the Free State and Northern Ireland ignored the claims of the nationalist majorities in areas just north of the border, but without the principle of nationality it is difficult to conceive of an Irish Free State. The principle of nationality was not invented during the First World War, but it took on a particular form that enabled the formation of small, independent nation-states across the continent between 1917 and 1922.

William Mulligan is a Professor of History at University College Dublin and author of The Great War for peace *(New Haven, 2014).*

Further reading

R. Crampton, *Aleksandur Stamboliiski* (Chicago, 2009).
N. Davies, *White eagle, red star: the Polish–Soviet War 1919–1920 and the Miracle on the Vistula* (London, 2003).
R. Gerwarth, *The vanquished: why the First World War failed to end* (London, 2016).

IRELAND AND POLAND 1919–21:
A BRIEF DIVERGENCE

BY **RÓISÍN HEALY**

Irish and Polish nationalists claimed that their countries were bound together by the experience of oppression at the hands of their respective neighbours. Poland and Ireland had indeed followed remarkably similar political trajectories from the 1790s, when failed uprisings resulted in a substantial loss of sovereignty, to the end of the First World War in 1918. An uprising led by the Polish noble Tadeusz Kościuszko in 1794 had prompted Prussia, Russia and Austria to annex the remainder of the Commonwealth of Poland-Lithuania, which they had already subjected to two annexations since 1772. The suppression of the United Irish Rebellion in 1798 led to the Act of Union, which abolished Ireland's parliament in Dublin and subjected the country to tighter control from an often hostile government in London. For over a century afterwards, nationalists in Ireland and Poland alike fought, by both constitutional and revolutionary means, to gain independence or, at the very least, devolved government.

The First World War presented both nationalist movements with an opportunity to advance their causes. All the occupying powers were involved—Britain and Russia on the

Above: Polish volunteers in 1920. Poles were engaged in a military struggle over Poland's borders that would continue right up to 1921 and prove far more destructive than the contemporary conflict in Ireland. (Alamy)

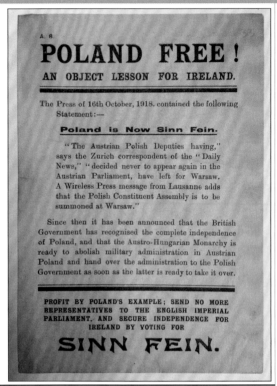

Entente side and Prussia and Austria on the other—and all boasted of their support for 'the rights of small nations'. Yet only Poland emerged from the war as an independent state. Poland had two substantial advantages that allowed it to steal a march on Ireland. The first of these was strong international support. In his Fourteen Points speech of January 1918, Woodrow Wilson singled out Polish independence and access to the sea as essential to a post-war peace settlement. Wilson's stance reflected a general consensus that the country had been badly treated and should be restored to statehood.

Irish nationalists could not draw on the same level of support. The fact that the majority of the Irish population spoke English rather than Irish, that Ireland was perceived not to have existed as an independent entity since the twelfth century and that Britain was widely regarded as a progressive power made the Irish case for independence unconvincing to many outside observers.

The second advantage that Poland enjoyed was the fate of the empires that had ruled it. All three had collapsed: Germany and Austria as a result of defeat in war, and

Russia by virtue of the turmoil that accompanied the Bolshevik Revolution. Poland emerged, alongside Czechoslovakia, Hungary and Yugoslavia, from the wreckage to become an independent state on 11 November 1918. The officer who supervised the withdrawal of German troops from occupied Poland, Harry Kessler, might have been struck by the stronger staying power of the British in Ireland. His mother was Alice Blosse Lynch, a member of the Anglo-Irish family of Partry House in Mayo, who had married a German banker.

Buoyed by the mandate given to Sinn Féin in the election of December 1918, Irish separatists did their best in the following years to place Ireland on the same footing as Poland. Irish leaders were very conscious of the need to cultivate international support and reached out to the Poles, among others. While excluded from the official proceedings of the Peace Conference, Irish nationalists went to Paris in 1919, and one of them, T.P. O'Connor, the MP for Liverpool, met privately with members of the National Polish Committee, who joined him in a toast to Irish freedom. In Ireland and Britain, nationalists used Britain's approval of Polish independence to press the case for independence for Ireland. All that was required to solve 'the Irish question', they asserted, was to extend the principle of self-determination from Poland to Ireland.

Yet the process of implementing self-determination in Poland proved far from straightforward. The principal difficulty was establishing the appropriate borders for the new state. It was a problem familiar to Irish observers, since partition had been mooted in discussions of the Third Home Rule Bill of 1912, but thornier because of Poland's greater diversity and geographical location at the heart of the continent. At its height, the Commonwealth had covered a vast amount of territory, including parts of present-day Lithuania, Latvia, Russia (Kaliningrad region), Belarus and Ukraine, and thus included many non-Poles. Poles and other ethnic groups were, moreover, often

dispersed over large areas. For instance, Poles formed ethnic enclaves in the eastern part of the former Commonwealth and were interspersed with German communities in the west, in a pattern similar to the demographic map of Ulster.

There was also a class dimension to relations between the different ethnic groups. In the east, Poles often occupied a higher socio-economic position, akin to that of the Anglo-Irish in Ireland. This ethnic diversity had posed few problems before 1795, but the increasing hold of nationalism across the region brought new challenges to Polish claims to dominance. The ambitions of other states in east-central Europe, both the Soviet Union and the states that emerged from the collapse of the region's empires, also proved problematic, as they sought territory claimed by the Polish government.

Even before the first shots rang out in the Irish War of Independence in January 1919, Poles were engaged in a military struggle over Poland's borders which would continue right up to 1921 and prove far more destructive than the contemporary conflict in Ireland. Between the end of the First World War in 1918 and 1921 there were no fewer than four uprisings led by Polish paramilitaries and four wars involving the new Polish state. The context for the uprisings was the struggle between Germans and Poles over the border between a truncated German state and the new Polish state. In December 1918 the Poles of the province of Poznania (or Posen) launched an attack on the remnants of the German army in order to ensure that the province, despite its one-third German population, would be awarded to the new Polish state at the Paris Peace Conference. Polish forces ousted the Germans and had their victory confirmed by the Treaty of Versailles.

The treaty also allowed Poland access to the Baltic Sea. This was a controversial point, since the so-called corridor created between Germany and its outlying province of East Prussia contained many German-speakers. The French diplomat Jules Cambon justified the transfer on the grounds that the Germans were not native to the region but had colonised it. Irish nationalists, challenging efforts to formalise partition in Ireland, were quick to assert an analogy with the Unionist community in Ulster and argued that the latter's presence was no justification for denying the island as a whole independence. Oblivious to the implications for Ulster, the Poles considered access to the Baltic essential to the economic viability of the new state and its achievement a cause for celebration. They marked it by a 'wedding to the sea' on 10 February 1920. At Puck, a town on the Baltic coast, the First World War hero General Józef Haller mounted a horse, rode into the sea and threw a ring into the water.

The Allied powers hoped to diffuse Polish–German antagonism elsewhere by means of plebiscites, whereby the inhabitants of disputed areas would vote on whether to remain in Germany or join the new Polish state. The campaigns that preceded the votes were characterised, however, by intimidation and violence. A plebiscite was first held in Allenstein and Marienwerder, parts of the provinces of East and West Prussia respectively, on 11 July 1920 and resulted in most territory remaining in Germany. A second plebiscite followed in Upper Silesia, an area highly prized for its extensive coal and iron ore deposits, located in the south-eastern tip of Germany. This campaign was particularly hard fought. Even before the plebiscite was held on 20 March 1921, Poles staged two uprisings against the German authorities and, after the plebiscite delivered most of

Above right: Józef Pildukski, who commanded Polish military forces in the several wars that wracked the new state between 1919 and 1921.

Right: A Sinn Féin leaflet in 1918 suggests that the pope will support both Polish and Irish independence. (NLI)

Opposite page: 'POLAND FREE'—during the 1918 general election a republican leaflet draws attention to Polish independence. (NLI)

F. 22.

THE POPE
AND
Full Independence

His Holiness Pope Benedict XV., writing on November 6th, 1918, to His Grace the Archbishop of Warsaw, said:—

"In the grave period through which Europe is now passing I am unable to resist showing my affection for the noble Polish Nation. . . . . Thanks be to God, the dawn of the resurrection of Poland is now finally waking. **Once Poland has regained her Full Independence, that she may again take up her place in the community of nations and resume her career as a civilising and Christian force is our most ardent prayer.**"

It is in **your** hands to earn for the noble Irish Nation such a tribute from His Holiness. It is only when Ireland "has regained her full independence" that she, too, will "again take up her place in the community of nations and resume her career as a civilising and Christian force."

WILL YOU VOTE FOR THE FULL INDEPENDENCE WHICH THE POPE BLESSED THE POLES FOR SECURING?

the territory (including many industrial districts) to Germany, a third Polish uprising took place to challenge the result. Eventually, the League of Nations had to arbitrate and awarded the bulk of the industrial districts to Poland.

While people in Ireland were preoccupied with their own War of Independence, some Irishmen gained the opportunity to study the German–Polish conflict at close quarters. As a signatory to the Versailles Treaty, Britain committed troops to keep the peace during the plebiscite campaigns. The Royal Irish Regiment was stationed in the Allenstein region for six months in 1920 and in Upper Silesia the following year. Wary of their loyalty to the British in the context of the Anglo-Irish War, the army command sent the Second Connaught Rangers and Second Leinster Regiment to join the Royal Irish in Upper Silesia. The German–Polish conflict might well have reminded Irish soldiers of the Anglo-Irish War raging at home. Indeed, an officer present explained the Silesian conflict to Sir Henry Wilson, the chief of the Imperial General Staff and originally from Longford, by identifying the Poles as Sinn Féin, the German self-defence units as the Ulster Volunteer Force and the Allied forces as the British army. Where the loyalties of the Irish troops lay in either the Irish or the Polish conflicts is unclear, however.

●

Above: Polish army defences near Milosna, west of Warsaw, during the war with the Soviets, August 1920.

Another officer, General Percy Radcliffe, asked Wilson to remove the First Battalion of the Royal Irish Regiment from Allenstein because, he claimed, they were 'full of Sinn Féin and cannot be relied on nor is their conduct doing any good to our prestige'. A few members of the regiment were reported to have caused 'a lot of trouble' when they visited the dentist in Gdańsk, a heavily German city. At the same time, the Royal Irish also included figures like Jack Morrogh, who had been involved in the suppression of the Easter Rising—he had taken down the 'Irish Republic' flag from the General Post Office—and was to be run out of Ireland by the Cork IRA in 1921.

Morrogh was one of many victims of the Anglo-Irish War, but it should be emphasised that the level of violence in Poland far exceeded that in Ireland in the same period. Historian Tim Wilson has established that fatalities in Upper Silesia between 1918 and 1922 amounted to 2,824, or 12.39 per 10,000 of the population, compared with 714 in Ulster, or 4.51 per 10,000. Moreover, he points out that the conflict in Upper Silesia was more vicious than in Ireland, involving the rape of women, the torture of prisoners, the mutilation of corpses and the denial of a decent burial. He ascribes the difference to the fact that the ethnic divisions in Upper Silesia were based on language rather than religion—both the Germans and the Poles were overwhelmingly Catholic. Identity in Upper Silesia was thus more fluid and

could be shifted with the exercise of extreme force. Religious conversion was a much bigger demand, and thus maintaining the loyalty of each side in Ulster was a task that required less violence.

The violence employed, often successfully, by the new Polish state on its other borders also raised tensions. While Poland was the victim of an attack by Czechoslovakia, which resulted in the transfer of a portion of Silesia to its neighbour, its other military engagements in these years were driven by a desire to expand its borders. The new state took up the Polish side in a struggle between Poles and Ukrainians over the ethnically mixed area of eastern Galicia, which began in early November 1918, and secured the area for Poland with Allied approval in mid-1920. It pressed its advantage and managed to push the border with the Soviet Union 200km beyond the Curzon Line agreed at the Paris Peace Conference after repulsing the Soviets at the so-called 'Miracle on the Vistula' in Warsaw in August 1920. Poland also annexed the city of Vilnius in a war against the newly created Lithuanian state in April 1919.

Lloyd George repeatedly expressed his exasperation with the Poles in these years by comparing them with troublemakers closer to home—the Irish. Only after the Anglo-Irish Treaty, however, did Irish nationalists come to (re)assert a parallel between the two peoples, not as troublemakers but as citizens of independent states making their way in a much-changed Europe.

Róisín Healy is Senior Lecturer in Modern European History at NUI Galway.

Further reading

R. Healy, *Poland in the Irish nationalist imagination: anti-colonialism within Europe* (London, 2017).
G. Barry, E. Dal Lago & R. Healy (eds), *1916 in global context* (Abington, 2017).
T. Wilson, *Frontiers of violence: conflict and identity in Ulster and Upper Silesia, 1918–1922* (Oxford, 2010).

'VERY DANGEROUS PLACES':

IRA GUNRUNNING AND THE POST-WAR UNDERWORLD

BY **BRIAN HANLEY**

Between 1919 and 1921 the IRA fought its war as a woefully under-equipped force. In mid-1921 it possessed just over 3,000 rifles, 5,000 handguns and around 60 machine-guns. Even then there were often mismatches of arms and ammunition.

Though it also had 15,000 shotguns, these figures are testament to its lack of modern arms. With over 70,000 Volunteers on its rolls, the IRA had far more men than guns. Many operations, especially in the early stages of the war, were largely concerned with capturing weapons. While GHQ sought various means of alleviating this problem, units continually complained of being under-equipped. Desperation for arms would ultimately lead local companies to seek their own sources of supply. Some republican leaders, including Harry Boland, were aware that their comparative military weakness meant that it was necessary to build 'a world-wide organisation ... whereby we can meet the enemy not alone in Ireland but all over the globe ... To Australia, Canada, South Africa, India, Egypt and Moscow our men must go to make common cause against our common foe.'

Post-war Europe was awash with modern weaponry. As armies demobilised and conflict erupted across much of the continent, the illicit arms trade boomed. Procuring weapons was one problem, however; getting them to Ireland was another. As IRA Quartermaster-general Seán McMahon asserted, 'the purchase of materials is a simple matter compared with our transport difficulties'. He explained how bringing just 100 rifles to Ireland involved 'first, the clearance from a foreign port where you have enemy agents always on the alert, then on arrival at an Irish port, you have even a closer net to get through, where every boat is carefully searched immediately on arrival. When you have them landed and distributed, what does it amount to? Merely two weapons per Brigade. It is a tough job to get one hundred weapons but it looks nothing when the Brigade gets its share.'

In order to alleviate these problems, ambitious plans were made for large arms consignments from Italy, the Soviet Union, Germany and the United States. A huge shipment, including 20,000 rifles and 500 machine-guns, was to come from Italy to the Munster IRA during the spring of 1921. When the operation was cancelled at short notice, it led to disappointment and recrimination. There were elaborate plans for importing the new Thompson machine-gun from America in the same year. The capture of 495 Thompsons at Hoboken, New Jersey, in June 1921 was a major blow.

●

Above left: Harry Boland speaks at Fenway Park, Boston, in 1920. A public figure during his time in the US, Boland was also a key organiser of attempts to supply arms, including the Thompson gun, to Ireland. (NLI)

machine-guns, 96 rifles and 520 handguns into Ireland. Though this figure is probably an underestimate, as units jealously guarded their supplies, it indicates how difficult a task gunrunning was. The majority of the IRA's arms arrived in small quantities, smuggled by individuals. Republican networks based at port cities were thus vital, with activists working in Hamburg and Antwerp, Southampton and London, and New York, New Orleans, St Johns and Montreal.

Liverpool was a key centre for both smuggling and transatlantic contacts. As one activist recalled in 1953, it 'was the most important port for communications between Dublin and America and the Continent. The Liners plying between Liverpool and New York, especially the White Star and Cunard Boats, had Irishmen aboard who were employed to take dispatches from Liverpool for New York.' Éamon de Valera, Liam Mellows, Harry Boland and Patrick McCartan were among those republicans spirited to America through Liverpool. There was a long-standing IRB organisation on Merseyside, which included seamen and dockers. Arms dumps were situated in areas of Irish population adjacent to the port. In London the IRA also operated around the docks, opening a shop in Royal Mint Street as a 'dump and collecting base' for weapons. A special unit of the Dublin Brigade, 'Q' Company, was organised among stevedores and other dockers to facilitate smuggling.

Post-war Britain was itself potentially fertile ground for republican efforts. Senior London policeman Sir Wyndham Childs worried about the 'thousands of rifles, machine guns, revolvers, Mills grenades, shells … lying about in dumps', warning that 'the IRA [might] have secured enough ammunition to have kept their body on its legs for years'. Republicans purchased weapons from British, Imperial or American servicemen (sometimes former comrades of theirs, as a significant number of

British Intelligence noted that 'the purchase of these weapons must have cost Sinn Féin a considerable amount of money which can ill be afforded'. The British were also

● Top: The Model 1921 Thompson gun, one of about 50 supplied to the IRA. Nearly 500 of the guns were impounded by US authorities before they could be shipped to Ireland in June 1921. (NMI)

● Above: From the BBC television series *Peaky Blinders*—Thomas Shelby (Cillian Murphy) toting a Lewis machine-gun, part of a consignment of weapons the Blinders stole from the local BSA factory and which the authorities feared would fall into the hands of communists or the IRA. In fact, the IRA did try to steal weapons from Birmingham's BSA factory. (BBC)

● Opposite page: Liverpool docks, c. 1920. Liverpool was regarded as the most important port for the IRA, as the liners plying between Liverpool and New York, especially the White Star and Cunard boats, had Irishmen aboard who were employed to take dispatches.

relieved 'that very few of these guns have reached the rebels'. In fact almost 50 had, but they came too late to have an impact on the war. Shipments from Germany, where front companies were established and boats purchased by republicans, proved more successful. German material reached Ireland both before and after the Truce, but a large amount of money was lost in confusing circumstances.

Though there were contacts with the Soviets throughout the period, the signing of a treaty with Britain by the Russians in 1921 scuppered republican hopes for support from the Soviet Union. In its search for arms the IRA was politically promiscuous, working with Bolsheviks, right-wing Germans, Italian irredentists and anyone else who might be helpful. Nevertheless, between August 1920 and July 1921 the IRA managed to smuggle just six

IRA activists were war veterans). One Manchester IRA man suggested that 'there could not have been much of a check by the British Army authorities on these guns judging by the rather easy way they could be disposed of'.

IRA Volunteers also carried out arms raids, stealing 50 rifles from an Australian army depot in Chelsea on one occasion. They utilised their contacts among mining communities in Lancashire and Scotland to procure explosives. They were occasionally aided by British radicals, who sometimes had no Irish connections. Republicans also made contact with revolutionaries from Britain's other imperial possessions. While dozens of republicans, both male and female, were engaged in this work, the quantities smuggled to Ireland still tended to be small. As the war intensified, IRA units in Ireland often reached out independently to emigrants from their native counties living in England and sought new means of gaining supplies.

Kilkenny native James Delaney was a London-based veteran of the Great War. During 1920 he was radicalised by the hunger strikes undertaken by republicans in Wormwood Scrubs, one of whom was a fellow Kilkenny man, Tom Treacy. Delaney visited Treacy in hospital, and Treacy asked him to help acquire arms for the Kilkenny IRA. With £100 provided by the Kilkenny IRA, Delaney sought out arms dealers with the assistance of two former London policemen, both Irish, who had been sacked because of their involvement in the 1919 police strike. They put Delaney in contact with a bookmaker named Conroy, a London Irishman with criminal connections. Conroy introduced Delaney to Ginger Barnett, a Jewish criminal, and a mixed-race gang leader known as 'Darby the Coon'. Barnett and Darby accompanied Delaney to maritime lodging houses in the East End, where he was able to purchase revolvers from African and Chinese sailors. As he was operating among a 'rough element of society' in 'very dangerous places',

Delaney received protection from a fellow war veteran (also a Kilkenny native) who had been a successful Royal Navy boxer. Dozens of handguns were supplied to the Kilkenny IRA until police arrested Delaney in November 1920.

Other London republicans were able to utilise similar networks. Denis Kelleher's best contact was 'a Jew named "Ginger" [who] lived near Whitechapel station … He was our main source of supply and he would deal only with myself. I had to go there 2 or 3 times a week, and we paid £2 or £3 a weapon.' Later on, Kelleher found a gunsmith in Hackney (also Jewish) who 'sold us any amount of stuff—Webleys … rifles and .303 and 45 ammunition'. Just as Delaney had sent arms to Kilkenny, Kelleher was solely involved in supplying the Cork No. 1 area. Owing 'to lack of resources', another London IRA man, Denis Carr, had initially 'only been able to pick up guns and ammunition in small quantities from returned soldiers'. Supplied with finance from Dublin, however, he was able to negotiate with, in his words, 'criminal gangs … such as "the Titanics" … the "Sabinis" of Clerkenwell, an Italian mob, and the Birmingham mob'. Through these contacts Carr was put in touch with what he called 'a crook arms dealer in the Hackney Road' and was 'able to tap

an unlimited source of ammunition and guns'.

Richard Walsh carried out extensive smuggling on behalf of the Mayo IRA, organising dumps for arms in Sheffield, Leeds, Liverpool and London. On occasion he swapped arms with other IRA units seeking weapons independently of GHQ. One of his London sources was the owner of a 'little bric-a-brac shop'. Walsh was unable to tell 'what race he belonged to', though 'he had at least a conversational knowledge of nine languages … this agent of ours was what was known as a "fence"—a dealer in stolen goods—and … jewelry was one of his specialties.' One of Walsh's depots was a pub in London's dockland, managed by a Jewish man whose Irish wife was a republican sympathiser.

James Cunningham, a Birmingham IRA member who had been held in Winson Green prison, recalled how 'the knowledge I gained of the underworld stood me in good stead, as it was a great source of "stuff"'. He never ventured into Birmingham's inner-city areas, however, without the aid of Dan O'Malley, an ex-soldier, partly for protection but also because he found the Birmingham accent impenetrable. The IRA also managed to attain three captured German machine-guns from a raid on a

depot in Gateshead. Gilbert Barrington (a war veteran and Labour activist) recalled that to move the guns 'a horse and cart had to be hired from a shady character … He was a member of a gang known as the Askew Road Gang, who were of the underworld type and I had to do the bargaining with him for the transportation of the goods.' In Sheffield, Joe Good recalled how 'we, at one time, rubbed shoulders of necessity with a criminal ring'.

Republicans were operating in cities in which there was considerable industrial and political turmoil, and where war veterans rubbed shoulders with political activists, immigrants and criminals. Ports were also rough environments, where smuggling and petty thieving formed part of everyday life. Many

●

Above: An IRA flying column in Connemara in 1921. The photograph is posed to suggest that the men are well equipped, but most IRA units suffered from chronic shortages of modern arms and ammunition. (UCD Archives)

among the IRA's maritime network came from this rough-and-tumble world. In Hamburg one contact was described as a 'bit of a booze hound [a] type that would do any job if paid for it'. Another sailor was said to be willing to 'do anything for money, was a gambler, and a general all round rough character'. A seaman who played an important role in helping to spirit de Valera to America 'cared for neither God nor man. One thing he liked, however … was to see the police get the worst of it always.'

The IRA in Ireland, in contrast, promoted a much more respectable image, and the Republican Police clamped down on crime. Nevertheless, by 1921 local units were increasingly carrying out armed robberies to raise funds for arms. This led to a new set of problems, as when, in County Mayo, the IRA robbed £5,000 from a local bank. Instead of being used to purchase arms, the money was divided up among some of those involved.

What is clear is that the IRA's

gunrunning network was becoming more streamlined and efficient. In the period between the Truce and the Treaty, republicans managed to import over 300 rifles, 600 handguns and 50 machine-guns, along with 90,000 rounds of ammunition. To do this, they had to display considerable ingenuity and flexibility, working on occasion with criminals as well as revolutionaries. This was not an aspect of the IRA's history that it acknowledged publicly, but it too played a part in the success of its efforts.

Brian Hanley's next book will be Loaded with dynamite: Ireland's global revolution 1916–1923.

Further reading

G. Noonan, *The IRA in Britain: 1919–1923* (Liverpool, 2014).

E. O'Connor, *Reds and the green: Ireland, Russia and the Communist Internationals* (Dublin, 2004).

H. Shore, *London's criminal underworlds, 1720–1930* (London, 2015).

'THE FUTURE OF FEMINISM':
THE IRISH WOMEN'S FRANCHISE LEAGUE AND THE WORLD REVOLUTION, 1917–20

BY **MAURICE J. CASEY**

In May 1920, members of the Irish Women's Franchise League (IWFL) gathered in Dublin to celebrate the approaching marriage of a dedicated member, Helen Yeates, to another supporter of their organisation, a young émigré from the former Russian Empire named Konrad Peterson. Maud Gonne gave a speech describing the symbolism of the coupling, later published in the journal tied to the IWFL, the *Irish Citizen*. This marriage, the indefatigable feminist noted, was 'symbolic of the closer union in the future between Ireland and Russia, two countries with such a strong spiritual kinship, and the only two which had successfully challenged the power of materialism and militarism during the war'. Gonne's framing of Ireland within a broader revolutionary context was not unusual for the time. Such an internationalist reading of Irish affairs was commonplace on the pages of the *Citizen* and in the meeting halls of the IWFL, where interest in the international revolutionary events that swept across post-war Europe was nurtured and transnational encounters were facilitated.

The recent centenary of partial franchise in Britain and Ireland raises the question: what came next for the politicised women who fought for the vote? In Ireland, the fight for independence from Britain provided an all-consuming cause for many women. For some, however, the national question was just one aspect of a broader, internationally inflected activism. As the Russo-Irish bridal shower described above indicates, national activity was often wedded to an international context. From the foundation of the IWFL in

Below: Members of the Irish Women's Franchise League in Hyde Park, London, in 1912. (Dublin City Library & Archive)

as inferior and that 'a new era will dawn for all people irrespective of race, creed or sex'. Shortly after Arnold wrote his first piece, the October Revolution inaugurated a programme of radical transformation. Enraptured by this new revolutionary turn, Arnold became the *Citizen*'s Bolshevik writer-in-residence.

In its annual round-up of events for 1917, the *Citizen* paid tribute to the Russian Revolution, describing it as 'one of the most energetic and enthusiastic fights which has ever been made by women themselves for their emancipation'. Irish women would play an important role in organising a reception committee to celebrate the Bolshevik programme. In February 1918 a committee was formed in Dublin to 'welcome the principles of the Russian Republic in the name of Irish democracy'. Margaret Connery of the IWFL and Maud Gonne were both vice-chairs. The committee staged a mass meeting wherein a lyrical resolution was passed, hailing 'with delight' the Bolshevik Revolution.

One of those who spoke at the meeting was the aforementioned Konrad Peterson, another Latvian emigrant who had taken part in demonstrations during the 1905 revolutionary wave in the Russian Empire and who would meet his future wife through IWFL circles. In a report on a Peterson lecture describing the New Russia to Irish feminists, the *Citizen* noted that he held the audience 'spellbound' as he traced the forces that made the revolution: the Russian people's 'long martyrdom', their deeply held desire for a democratic state and the 'noble part played by University students'. One year later, Peterson attended an IWFL summer pageant dressed as a Bolshevik. Unfortunately, the report of the pageant failed to outline what Dublin party-goers deemed recognisably Bolshevik fashion. These personal encounters with émigrés from the Russian Empire and identification with the ideals of the Russian Revolution provided Irish feminists with links to far-off events in an era

1908 until the *Citizen* ceased publication in 1920, its meeting halls hosted a social circle of feminists with connections to events and comrades abroad. On the pages of its journal can be read an alternative view of Irish revolutionary developments, one which described events in Ireland as sub-plots in a broader revolutionary narrative that linked insurrectionary cities such as Petrograd, Budapest and Berlin to hubs of rebel activity in London and Dublin.

For revolutionaries across the world who had lived through the slaughter of the war, the two revolutions which transformed Russia in 1917 were world-shaking events. The February Revolution was sparked by protests supported by soldiers, women and industrial workers, which brought down the Tsarist regime and installed a provisional government. Universal suffrage soon followed. Later that year,

after the October Revolution, Lenin ascended to power and declared Russia to be the world's first socialist state. Under the guidance of Bolshevik feminist Alexandra Kollontai, an unprecedented social programme designed to transform gender relations was initiated. Women in Ireland, who were seizing their own revolutionary opportunities to transcend traditional gender roles, took notice of events in distant Moscow and Petrograd.

From 1917 onwards, the *Citizen* began to cover Russian revolutionary affairs. Interestingly, the paper relied largely on a local emigrant community to provide the analysis. For the *Citizen*, which had opposed the Great War from a pacifist stance, the key point of interest in Russia was whether or not the newly ascendant powers would recognise the equality of men and women. It was on this topic that Sidney Arnold, a Latvian emigrant resident in Dublin, provided his first contribution to the *Citizen*. Assuming an authoritative stance by describing himself as a 'Russian citizen' attuned to the 'tendencies of the Russian idealists', Arnold proclaimed that his native revolutionaries did not see women

● Above: Sylvia Pankhurst addresses a (mostly male) crowd in Trafalgar Square, London, in 1909.

● Opposite page: *The Irish Citizen*—newspaper of the Irish Women's Franchise League.

before mass communication.

Another important Irish tie to the revolutionary world was the link between Irish feminists and the East London radical milieu centred around revered suffragette Sylvia Pankhurst. Founded as the East London Federation of Suffragettes in 1914 and headquartered at 400 Old Ford Road, this organisation would ultimately rename itself the Workers' Socialist Federation in 1917, as Pankhurst led her organisation towards the radical left of the political spectrum. It is unsurprising that the IWFL, the most militant of the Irish groups fighting for the vote, would associate with an organisation whose journal, the *Workers' Dreadnought*, carried the slogan 'Socialism, Internationalism, Votes for All' on its masthead. Yet behind the headlines of the *Dreadnought* existed a vibrant and woman-dominated social world that brought together Irish feminists, British socialists and international radicals.

Many of the women who inhabited IWFL social circles and debated feminism and nationalism in the pages of the *Citizen* were welcomed in Pankhurst's headquarters. One 1920 anti-Irish republican pamphlet decried Pankhurst's rooms as a 'nest of revolution', where Hanna Sheehy Skeffington could be found speaking 'under the Sinn Féin flag' to an audience of Russians. Although the pamphlet was sensational propaganda aimed at outlining a 'Sinn Fein–Bolshevist' conspiracy, there was a grain of truth to this charge. Several Irish women did lecture under Pankhurst's auspices. In 1919 Maud Gonne lectured at 400 Old Ford Road, describing Ireland as a missionary to the world, upholding a 'true conception of Freedom'. Expanding on her thoughts in the *Dreadnought*, Gonne referred to the 'great meeting in the Mansion House to welcome the Russian Republic', which had revealed to her a growing enthusiasm among the Irish people for what she termed a 'Social Cooperative Commonwealth'. Other Irish women who contributed to the *Dreadnought* included Nora

Connolly, daughter of James, and the poet and suffragist Eva Gore Booth.

This Dublin–East London rebel network was reciprocal. In May 1919 Sylvia Pankhurst arrived in the Irish capital to lecture on the merits of a Soviet-style political system. Prior to this meeting, Pankhurst visited the Limerick soviet, the famed general strike that saw nationalists occupy the city, print their own money and arrange the distribution of supplies.

Pankhurst's speech to the IWFL was duly preserved for the historical record by a superintendent dispatched to conduct surveillance on the feminist rabble-rouser. Under a soviet system, Pankhurst informed her audience in a Westmoreland Street meeting room, there would be no employers, everybody would receive equal wages and infant mortality rates would plummet. She held up the Limerick soviet as a model, and berated the Dublin audience for failing to express full solidarity with 'such a magnificent effort'. Her central contention was clear: the only way forward was 'the complete overthrow of capitalism'.

Members of the audience contested some of Pankhurst's points, asserting that Ireland had supported the Limerick strike and that any attempt to establish a co-operative society in the country would be thwarted by British force. Nevertheless, the meeting itself demonstrates the desire of Irish radicals for encounters with activists embedded in international revolutionary networks, and the role played by feminist organisations such as the IWFL in facilitating such encounters. Pankhurst would not be the last visiting radical to provide Irish audiences with a personal connection to revolutionary events abroad.

Although the Bolsheviks inspired a practice and language of insurrection that spread across the continent, it was not only the Russian Revolution that attracted the interest of Dublin feminists and

their associates. In September 1919 the *Citizen* reported on an address given to the Irishwomen's International League by Alice Riggs Hunt, a New York suffrage campaigner who visited the Hungarian soviet as part of a wider European tour. For 133 days a communist government ruled a large portion of Hungary. By the time of Hunt's lecture in Dublin the revolutionary government had already collapsed, but this did not deter the speaker from sharing her reflections on the system. Hunt noted that women and men had shared the same rations, teachers had their labour valued above all, and that the Red Guards, vilified in the Western press, had been 'kindly and helpful'. Reading her Irish audience well, Hunt discussed the pro-soviet contributions made by Hungarian women imprisoned for pacifist agitation during the war, noting that these women supported the 'temporary reliance' on physical force to defend the revolutionary government. A few months after Hunt's lecture, the Irish suffrage campaigner Lucy Kingston wrote in the *Citizen* of her hope that the world had not heard the last of 'the great experiment' that was the Hungarian soviet.

In Germany another revolution aimed at socialist transformation arose briefly in 1919 before its brutal suppression. Although no lecturer arrived in Dublin to educate the IWFL on the unrest in locations such as Berlin and Bavaria, the *Citizen* paid particular attention to the unfortunate demise of two central participants: Rosa Luxemburg and Karl Liebknecht. These two revolutionary socialists, who had opposed the war, were eventually murdered by paramilitaries on account of their insurrectionary activities. For the *Citizen*, the death of anti-war militants in state-sanctioned killings demonstrated a familiar pattern. When memorialising former editor Francis Sheehy Skeffington on the pages of the *Citizen*, the names of Liebknecht and Luxemburg were evoked alongside his, for they too were pacifists

who 'by their deaths have done more to discredit and destroy militarism than any act of their lives could have done'. While Francis Sheehy Skeffington is more often memorialised alongside Irish rebels, it is interesting to note that his own journal placed him within a pantheon of world revolutionaries.

But what was the path forward for women in Ireland? Addressing the IWFL on the topic of the 'Future of Feminism' in March 1919, Margaret Connery stated that their political progress lay in 'social revolutions' which, she argued, 'go nearer to the heart of things and affect the lives of women more closely than mere political revolutions'. Connery was evoking the contemporary language of world revolutionaries in Budapest, Petrograd and beyond, who were arguing not simply for radical political change but for the transformation of society itself. Following the 1918 Franchise Act, and in the wake of revolutionary change in Ireland, Russia and elsewhere, the networks of the international women's movement continued to fight for social justice, and many were fundamentally transformed by revolutionary attempts to expand contemporary political horizons. In the feminist meeting halls of Dublin, and on the pages of the *Citizen*, many Irish women and their comrades found a means of engaging with this world revolution.

Maurice J. Casey is a DPhil. student at Jesus College, University of Oxford.

Further reading

L. Ryan, *Winning the vote for women: the* Irish Citizen *newspaper and the suffrage movement in Ireland* (Dublin, 2018).

S. Pašeta, *Irish nationalist women, 1900–1918* (Cambridge, 2015).

M. Ward, *Hanna Sheehy Skeffington, suffragette and Sinn Féiner: her memoirs and political writings* (Dublin, 2017).

●

Left: Sylvia Pankhurst lectures in Dublin on the Russian Revolution, May 1919. (National Archives, UK)

FELLOW WORKERS! 12

At the Abbey Theatre on Sunday May 11th at 8 p.m. MR. SERGEITCH of the RUSSIAN LIBERATION COMMITTEE will, *so he says,* tell the "TRUTH ABOUT RUSSIA."

Ask him the truth about this little story printed in the orange circular "Notes from Ireland," & "Freeman's Journal"—

"A further statement issued by the RUSSIAN LIBERATION COMMITTEE, London, reports that the Council of People's Commisaries have voted 500,000,000 roubles (approximately £50,000,000) monthly from the Bureau of General Foreign Propaganda AND THAT THE FIRST PAYMENT OF 500,000,000 ROUBLES (for February) WAS SENT TO THE SINN FEINERS IN IRELAND. (See "The Times," 30th April 1919.)"

After he withdraws his Committee's slander on Ireland it will be time enough to hear his version of The "Truth about Russia."

Sylvia Pankhurst will be at the Abbey to tell the Story of the Revolution

SYLVIA PANKHURST (Of the "Workers' Dreadnought.")

Will lecture under the auspices of CUMANNACHT NA H-EIREANN on "RUSSIA TO-DAY."

in the Trades' Hall, Capel Street, on Monday next, May 12th AT 8 P.M.

ADMISSION FREE.   DISCUSSION.   COLLECTION.

Get your Ticket NOW for the Connolly Birthday Concert in the Mansion House, on Thursday, June 5th.   ::   Admission 1/-

Mitchell & Co., Printers, 29 Capel Street.

PROCLAIMING NATIONHOOD

Our dream is a world-wide organisation ... with a plan of campaign whereby we can meet the enemy not alone in Ireland but all over the globe. Thus only can Britain be shown the power of Ireland ... To Australia, Canada, South Africa, India, Egypt and Moscow our men must go to make common cause against our common foe.

——Harry Boland to Joseph McGarritty, New York, 3 August 1920

Image: Detail from a postcard showing 'Uncle Sam' ushering Ireland, in the form of a uniformed member of the Irish Volunteers, into the Paris peace conference. Hopes that the United States would support Irish claims for independence were, however, wildly optimistic. (NLI)

GLOBAL HORIZONS? THE IRISH QUEST FOR INTERNATIONAL RECOGNITION

BY **GERARD KEOWN**

At its first sitting, on 21 January 1919, Dáil Éireann adopted not just the Declaration of Independence but also a 'Message to the Free Nations of the World' in which the Dáil pledged to 'resume that intercourse with other peoples which befits us as a separate nation'.

The following day, the Dáil equipped itself with the external trappings of this newly acquired statehood, appointing Count George Plunkett, father of the executed 1916 rebel, as Minister for Foreign Affairs, and voted to dispatch envoys abroad to plead its case for recognition.

Envoys were sent to the capitals of Europe, across the United States, to South America and beyond over the next three years. Co-operation was forged with Indians, Egyptians and others seeking independence in the post-war world, while efforts were made to mobilise the Irish diaspora living abroad. A draft treaty was even negotiated with the Russian Bolsheviks in 1920. The Irish struggle was conducted on the international stage in a way never seen before.

In Dublin, a 'foreign ministry' was created to support these efforts, operating from a secret address. As in other clandestine Dáil offices, its officials would quickly disappear through a skylight or down a drainpipe when the Crown forces came calling, as they inevitably did.

After four years of war and upheaval in Europe, the international order was rapidly being reshaped, as movements that looked and sounded like Sinn Féin carved out new states. While the main focus was on efforts at home

to secure independence, republicans saw an opportunity to internationalise their case. In February 1919 the Dáil dispatched a future president of Ireland, Seán T. Ó Ceallaigh, to Paris to seek a hearing at the post-war peace conference. On arrival, he found the city's hotels overflowing with delegates, journalists, lobbyists and petitioners. As presidents and prime ministers took up residence, the French capital became the centre of world opinion. This was the first modern peace conference, played out before the world's press and public opinion, thanks to the global communications infrastructure of the day.

The city was also brimming with representatives of national groups and subject peoples, including Egyptians, Indians and a young Ho Chi Minh. Drawn by the words of President Woodrow Wilson and his internationalist vision, they hoped that the peacemakers would apply the principle of self-determination to them. There was considerable speculation about what would happen if the Irish attempted to present their case. It would not be as simple, however, as knocking on the door and asking for admission.

The reality was that Wilson had not been thinking of Ireland when he drafted his Fourteen Points, regarding the 'Irish question' as an internal British issue. Unsurprisingly, this was also the British view, and one shared by the French who were chairing the peace conference. With delegates busy pursuing their own goals, be it winning recognition for new states, grabbing colonial spoils or the elusive quest for security guarantees, it was not in anyone's interest to insist otherwise. Finding his overtures rebuffed, Ó Ceallaigh lamented that nobody wanted 'to listen to anyone like myself who wants justice and right to prevail'. Back in Dublin, the Sinn Féin newspaper *Nationality* portrayed the conference's participants as labouring hard to 'make the world safe for hypocrisy', as it became

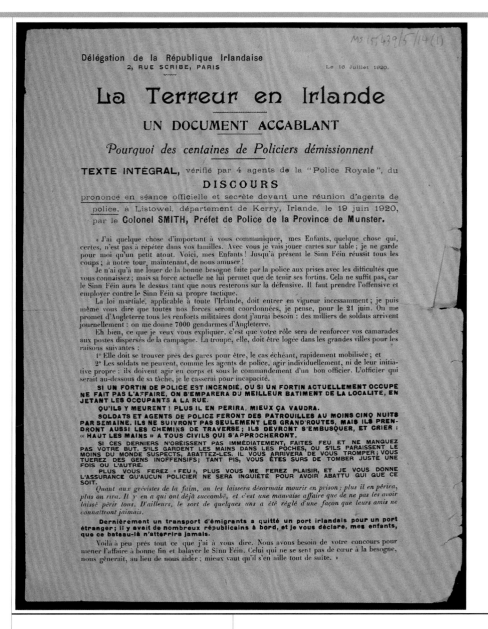

clear that the principle of self-determination would be applied selectively where it suited those who had won the war.

Irish republicans were also interested in Wilson's Fourteenth Point, a world League of Nations, the first organ of global governance that the peace conference would bring to life. Membership would constitute a seal of legitimacy for the newly minted states of Europe. In April 1919 the Dáil voted to seek membership in the League, and to accept 'all duties, responsibilities and burdens' which this implied. Ó Ceallaigh and his fellow envoy George Gavan Duffy, the barrister who had defended Roger Casement

in his 1916 treason trial, lobbied for admission in Paris. The League, however, would be a club of established states, and there was no Irish name-plate on the door when it met for the first time in January 1920.

●

Above: 'La Terreur en Irlande'—a French-language propaganda bulletin produced by the Sinn Féin delegation in Paris, 1920. (NLI)

●

Opposite page: Irish diplomats in Paris, including George Gavan Duffy (foreground) and Seán T. Ó Ceallaigh (second from left). Ó Ceallaigh would lament that at Versailles nobody would 'listen to anyone like myself who wants justice and peace to prevail'. (NLI)

K. 4.

DO YOU WANT PRESIDENT WILSON'S HELP AT THE PEACE CONFERENCE?

YOU CAN HAVE IT IF YOU ASK FOR IT AS A SMALL NATION WHICH DEMANDS THE RIGHT TO INDEPENDENCE.

IF YOU ASK FOR IT AS A PEOPLE READY TO ACCEPT HOME RULE WITHIN THE BRITISH EMPIRE, HE CAN ONLY SAY: "YOU CHOOSE THE BRITISH EMPIRE AS YOUR RULERS. GO ASK A SETTLEMENT FROM THEM; YOU HAVE TIED MY HANDS. IT IS NO LONGER MY AFFAIR."

President Wilson's object is to Free Subject Nations, not to establish English garrisons in English Colonies.

THEN VOTE SO THAT PRESIDENT WILSON MAY HAVE OVERWHELMING PROOF OF IRELAND'S DEMAND TO BE FREE.

Despite the disappointment of the peace conference, support would remain among many Irish nationalists for a broad internationalist vision as the best means of guaranteeing the rights of small states, including

● Above: 'DO YOU WANT PRESIDENT WILSON'S HELP AT THE PEACE CONFERENCE?'—a Sinn Féin leaflet from the 1918 general election. (NLI)

● Opposite page: Patrick McCartan and Liam Mellows, republican emissaries in America from 1917. McCartan was the key link between the Dáil and the Bolsheviks. (NMI)

Ireland. With the signing of the Treaty of Versailles on 28 June 1919, however, Paris ceased to offer a forum for activity, and the focus then shifted to seeking recognition from individual countries.

Éamon de Valera arrived in the United States in June and embarked on a countrywide tour. Crowds greeted him everywhere he went, in an ambitious programme masterminded by his lieutenants Harry Boland and Patrick McCartan. Such was the throng of well-wishers, de Valera quipped, that he would

have the biceps of a blacksmith. But it was his skills as an orator that were put to work, generating civic petitions and acres of newsprint.

Despite initial success in winning supportive resolutions in both houses of Congress, further progress was blocked by internal dissent among Irish republicans. At issue was a question that would bedevil early attempts to engage with the Irish diaspora in the United States and elsewhere: should Irish-American leaders take the lead in the campaign for recognition or take their cue from the Irish at home?

Disagreement over this question split the Irish organisation in America in 1920, and de Valera failed to secure a pledge from either the Democratic or Republican parties to support Irish independence in that year's general election. As the popular appetite for monster rallies faltered after a year on the road, it became clear that Washington was not going to recognise a rebel Irish republic. De Valera returned home empty-handed in December 1920.

Efforts in the meantime were being pursued on the other side of the Atlantic, where George Gavan Duffy and Ó Ceallaigh led a network of Sinn Féin envoys across Europe. While some sympathy for republicans existed in France, Italy and Germany, for different reasons there was little inclination on the part of European countries to become involved. The French remembered Irish republicans' links to Germany, the Germans had their hands full managing domestic instability and the Italians had their own troubles at home. Contact with the new states of Eastern Europe was almost non-existent.

Republican efforts at the Vatican were focused on averting a hostile stance towards Irish aspirations or the methods being used to achieve them at home. With the threat of clerical condemnation of Sinn Féin a very real danger in 1920, recognition was never formally requested, as it was understood that it would not be forthcoming.

The reality of British power and influence made engaging with Irish separatism an unattractive proposition for any foreign government. For this reason, some argued that the focus should be on fostering cooperation with Indians, Egyptians and others who sought independence from the British Crown. But while contacts were established (as Kate O'Malley explores elsewhere in this issue, pp 79–83), the scope was limited and plans for a league of subject peoples did not get off the ground.

The strangest episode in the Dáil's efforts to win recognition is the story of the agreement it negotiated with the Bolsheviks. The IRB discussed the idea of sending Patrick McCartan to Russia in 1917, but as conditions were not right at that time he went to Washington instead. By 1919 contacts had been established between Sinn Féin and the Russians in New York, and talks soon followed on a possible co-operation agreement between the two. The idea of sending McCartan to Russia was revived the following year, this time to finalise the talks, but he would not arrive in Moscow until St Valentine's Day 1921. By then the Russians had gone cold on the idea of a treaty, and McCartan left empty-handed in June.

Why did Sinn Féin embrace the Bolshevik bear? Events in revolutionary Russia were followed in Ireland with as much interest but as little understanding as elsewhere. It was hoped that a deal would pressure the British, provide arms for the war in Ireland and result in a propaganda victory. Cooler heads pondered the impact on a public opinion, at home and abroad, fearful of Bolshevism and its spread.

No country had recognised the Irish Republic by the time negotiations began for what would become the Anglo-Irish Treaty of December 1921. Sinn Féin stopped short of requesting recognition from the United States or any other government. It was a step constantly under consideration but circumstances never seemed quite right. Were ideas of foreign policy

and international affairs part of many people's thinking? Was the appeal to the Paris Peace Conference conceived as a piece of political theatre, an alternative to Westminster or a strategy to internationalise the Irish question? Whatever the motives, the campaign for international recognition forced some in the nationalist movement to think about international politics for the first time.

Intended as a stirring appeal for recognition, the 'Message to the Free Nations' was also a diplomatic manifesto of sorts, setting out a first geopolitical vision for Ireland:

'Internationally, Ireland is the gateway of the Atlantic. Ireland is the last outpost of Europe towards the West: Ireland is the point upon which great trade routes between East and West converge: her independence is demanded by the Freedom of the Seas: her great harbours must be open to all nations …'

Undeniably a document of its time, there is a modern ring to some of its language, with its references to 'freedom and justice as the fundamental principles of international law', 'frank co-operation between the peoples for equal rights', and its belief in the principles of self-determination as the only basis for a lasting peace 'by establishing the control of government in every land upon the basis of the free will of a free people'.

The Cork academic John J. Horgan offered a similarly beguiling economic rationale for independence, describing Ireland as 'the natural European base for American commerce', with its harbours providing 'the front door to the European markets'. These and other imaginings of Ireland's place in the world were repeated in numerous pamphlets, documents and statements during the republic's three-year campaign for international recognition. It was even suggested that an independent Ireland could become the 'first of the small nations'.

Differing identities were pressed into service as occasion suited: that of the moral people, whether its roots be Christian or Gaelic; that of the insulated island untouched by the failings of diplomacy or the modern world; that of the disinterested nation able to act as go-between; that of the mother country, with a diaspora

● Above: Lenin with (to his right) Irish communist Roddy Connolly, Moscow, 1920—while the Irish left sought support from the Soviets, Dáil Éireann agreed a draft treaty with the Bolsheviks in 1920 but it was never formally ratified.

across the English-speaking world; and that of the wronged people, whose redress would anoint a new era of open diplomacy and self-determination.

Through an act of political alchemy, being an outsider, on the periphery, became an asset. Many believed that an Irish state would have no selfish national interests and so could act as bridge-builder or honest broker, speaking freely on the international issues of the day. Such undiplomatic frankness, it was assumed, would be welcomed in the new era of open diplomacy. Others viewed the workings of the diplomatic chessboard with mistrust, Eoin MacNeill, leader of the Irish Volunteers in 1916, warning against outcomes born of 'wining, dining and undermining'. Few paused to consider whether geopolitical irrelevance might befall an independent Irish state.

If some of the language used conveyed the impression of a country outside the European mainstream, this was not the case. Sinn Féin and its precursor, the National Council, were present at transnational gatherings of stateless peoples in The Hague in 1907, London in 1910, Paris in 1915 and

New York in 1917. The international suffrage movement (as Maurice Casey's essay highlights, pp 27–30) exposed Irish women and some men to fresh currents of thought, while Catholic internationalism and a fear of Bolshevism motivated others. Others were influenced by a wider European discussion on the role of the nation and the state, their relationship with each other, and Ireland's rights and obligations as members of a newly conceived international community of states.

There is something modern about the aspiration to a foreign policy based on beliefs rather than the pursuit of selfish interests, even if the Irish state would ultimately prove to have interests and to pursue them. Equally modern was an attempt to create an international rationale for Irish independence and an appeal to the international community. There was also a keen appreciation of the value of harnessing the power of public opinion in international affairs.

If Sinn Féin's propaganda efforts abroad ultimately failed to secure recognition of the Republic, their greater significance lies in the fact that some Irish nationalists were thinking about the international environment, its impact on Ireland and how goals at home could be pursued by pursuing them abroad. Some of these ideas would shape Irish foreign policy once independence had been achieved, while the new state's fledgling diplomatic service would trace its roots to the network of amateur envoys dispatched by the Dáil in 1919.

Gerard Keown is an Irish civil servant and diplomat.

Further reading

M. Kennedy *et al.* (eds), *Documents in Irish Foreign Policy, Vol. 1: 1919–1922* (Dublin, 1998).

D. Keogh, *Ireland and Europe, 1919–1989* (Cork, 1990).

G. Keown, *First of the small nations: the beginnings of Irish foreign policy 1919–1932* (Oxford, 2016).

'SOMETHING TYPICALLY IRISH AS WELL AS ESSENTIALLY MODERN':

THE IRISH BOND DRIVE IN THE UNITED STATES

BY **ROBIN J.C. ADAMS**

De Valera stepped out of the Waldorf Astoria onto New York's Park Avenue on 17 January 1920. His car left the Waldorf at noon, followed by a motorcade festooned with Irish tricolours. Heralded by a pipe band playing 'rousing Irish airs', he alighted at City Hall, where he was greeted by a throng of people. On de Valera's arrival, State Senator William Bourke Cockran, a former fund-raiser for John Redmond, presented the 'President of Ireland' to the mayor of New York. In an outdoor ceremony, de Valera received the freedom of the city from the mayor, who then very publicly purchased the first 'bond certificate' of the Irish Republic. This ceremony marked the launch of the First External Loan, or 'bond drive' as it came to be known, an ambitious fund-raising campaign that targeted the Irish diaspora in the United States. Along with the National Loan, its domestic Irish equivalent, the American bond drive provided the Dáil with the financial means to prosecute the War of Independence.

In a statement combining legalese with the language of statehood, de Valera proceeded to

Below: A 'republican bond' sold to raise money for the Dáil in the United States in January 1920. (NLI)

Above: Henry Ford—the British consul general in New York believed, 'on fairly reliable authority', that the motor magnate had given a personal guarantee to cover any shortfall to the bond drive's $10m target.

explain the terms of the bond drive to the reporters assembled at City Hall:

'It will be distinctly understood by each subscriber to the loan that he is making a free gift of his money. Repayment of the amount subscribed is contingent wholly upon the recognition of the Irish Republic as an independent nation. Each member will receive a certificate of indebtedness of the republic, signed by myself, or my deputy, which certificate is non-negotiable and non-interest-bearing. The certificate will be exchangeable on par for gold bonds of the republic upon presentation at the treasury of the republic after freedom is obtained. The gold bonds will bear 5 per cent interest from the date of the recognition of the republic and will be redeemable at par one year from the same date.'

While apparently novel, the idea of selling bonds to raise money for an unrecognised state was by no means a new one. Louis Kossuth, the Hungarian nationalist fêted by Arthur Griffith in *The resurrection of Hungary* (1904), toured America in 1852 selling his 'Hungary Bonds', as did Gottfried Kinkel, leader of the failed Baden revolution in Germany. The American adventurer William 'Filibuster' Walker sold bonds of the 'Republic of Nicaragua' in 1856 to fund the creation of an English-speaking colony there. Indeed, the Dáil's own antecedents, the Fenian Brotherhood, sold bonds of the 'Irish Republic' in America to fund their ill-fated 'invasion of Canada' in 1866. Neither was the Dáil the only unrecognised government collecting money in America at the time. Representatives of the Lithuanian Republic were also in America selling bonds in 1920, and memories were fresh of the Czechoslovak and Polish governments in exile soliciting donations from their diasporas in America during the war. Of course, the best-known precedent for the average American would have been the US government's Liberty Loan campaigns of 1917–18, an association the bond drive's organisers sought to exploit.

The Dáil's bond certificates were issued in denominations of $10, $25, $50, $100, $250, $500, $1,000, $5,000 and $10,000. The smaller amounts were designed to attract subscriptions from as many people as possible, in order to demonstrate popular support, while the larger ones were printed for use in propaganda. Certificates for $10 were to be paid in cash in a single instalment; certificates of $25 and over were to be paid 25% on application, 25% in 30 days, 25% in 60 days, and 25% in 90 days. Linking the bond drive to the older tradition of advanced nationalist fund-raising in America, the Dáil mission accepted Fenian bonds at par in exchange for Dáil bonds. The *Financial Times* described this arrangement as 'something typically Irish as well as essentially modern', although it also noted: 'A less sentimental and idealistic people would certainly have deemed it wise to forget that 1866 issue'. Perhaps to counter the perceived riskiness of the Fenian bonds, bonds of the US Treasury's Liberty Loans were also accepted at par, implying parity of credibility between the two republics while also linking the Dáil's claims for recognition to President Wilson's war aim of independence for small nations.

De Valera's reception at City Hall marked the beginning of 'Irish Loan Week', a ten-day period from 17 to 26 January 1920 which set in motion a promotional campaign that spanned the country. The day after his reception at City Hall, de Valera took to the stage of New York's Lexington Theater. The bond drive organisers for the city's boroughs pledged to raise more than $2.5m, and de Valera was reportedly cheered for nearly five minutes by the almost 3,000 supporters in attendance. The receipt of a cheque from Archbishop Patrick Hayes of New York for $1,000 was announced on stage, and the archbishop and New York Governor Alfred E. Smith sent strong letters of endorsement of the loan. Rabbi David Klein also spoke, equating the Irish struggle with the Jewish demand for a national homeland, a sentiment that was repeated in a number of other rallies.

The first days of the bond drive were intense. While de Valera was accepting the freedom of New York, Harry Boland and others were busy promoting the loan in Chicago. The following day, they addressed an 'immense' meeting at the Academy of Music in Philadelphia. On 21 January 1920, about 12,000 people turned out to welcome de Valera in Albany, where he addressed a session of the New York State legislature. The assembly had passed a unanimous resolution approving of the issue of bond certificates two days earlier, recommending them to the American people. Staying in New York, the next day de Valera held meetings in Richmond Hill, Jamaica, Flushing and Long Island City.

The bond drive was also pushed forward on the ground,

facilitated by Irish-American organisations such as the Friends of Irish Freedom. As observed by the British consul general, 'Posters appeared in all the principal places in New York advocating the American form of government for Ireland'. Emphasising the Dáil's democratic credentials, these posters showed 'by large coloured maps, the proportion of Sinn Féin and other parties in the 1918 election'. Young women were seen selling bond certificates in the lobbies of some of New York's most prominent hotels, imitating tactics used in the Liberty Loan campaigns. In Boston, the *Irish Press* reported a series of 'noonday street rallies', where 'Colleens in costume rode in a big decorated auto truck through the principal streets', with music of all sorts blaring. Even in St Louis, Missouri, the British consul reported that windows in the houses of a number of residential areas were displaying green, white and orange posters with the words 'Subscriber Irish Bond Certificates'. Adverts were also taken out in the press, and those newspapers owned by William Randolph Hearst were particularly enthusiastic in their coverage. 'No matter what your opinions may be of the hopefulness of … such an establishment as an Irish Republic,' reflected New York's *Evening World*, 'you cannot help but understand the human side of this singularly interesting drive.'

The bond drive was not without its critics, however. The Wall Street press was particularly hostile. The *Wall Street Journal* warned that anyone who purchased the bond certificates could not be guaranteed any return, and this sentiment was repeated elsewhere. The financial editor of the *New York Tribune* advised its readers not to exchange Liberty Bonds for 'so-called Irish bonds', which they described as 'one of the most highly speculative "securities" ever offered to the American public'. Perhaps the most scathing of reactions to the bond drive came from an editorial in the Wall Street publication *The Street*, which was reprinted in the *New York Times* and picked up by

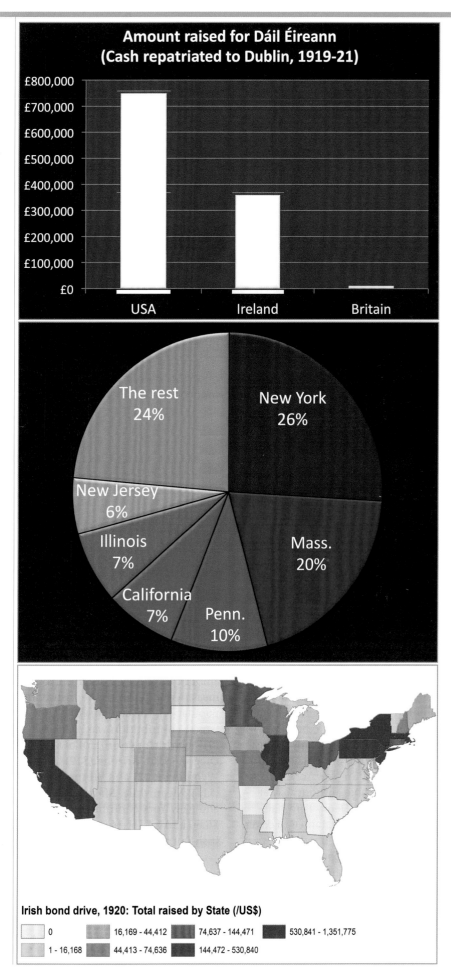

Amount raised for Dáil Éireann (Cash repatriated to Dublin, 1919-21)

Irish bond drive, 1920: Total raised by State (/US$)

| 0 | 16,169 - 44,412 | 74,637 - 144,471 | 530,841 - 1,351,775 |
| 1 - 16,168 | 44,413 - 74,636 | 144,472 - 530,840 | |

the *Daily Telegraph* in London. Referring to 'this absurd but dangerous Irish Loan swindle', the editorial asserted that 'no intelligent patriotic American will give them the money they wish to shoot British policemen in the back or attempt assassination of British officials in Ireland'.

The British government's representatives in the United States kept a watchful eye on the activities of the bond drive organisers, as embassy and consulates wrote numerous reports on their activities. The Foreign Office was slow to react, however, taking the view that the drive would probably be a failure. Moreover, anxious to renegotiate British war debt to America, Lloyd George was wary of making any statements that could rile public opinion in a US presidential election year. Of some concern, however, was the involvement of American business in the bond drive. The British consul general in New York believed, 'on fairly reliable authority', that motor magnate Henry Ford had given a personal guarantee to cover any shortfall to the bond drive's $10m target. The consul general suspected that Standard Oil was also

●

Above: Daniel Day Lewis playing Edward L. Doheny, the Californian oil baron and inspiration for the movie *There will be blood*, who subscribed $10,000.

affording 'considerable financial support' to Irish agitation in America in order to court Irish-American politicians in Washington. However, although there were certainly interactions between members of these businesses and the Dáil's mission to America, and de Valera did indeed meet Ford to discuss matters of politics, there is no evidence of material support from either source for the bond drive.

After nine months of campaigning, the bond drive closed for new subscriptions on 14 October 1920, having raised $5,151,800 from 276,219 subscribers. According to historian Francis Carroll, this was the largest amount ever raised by the Irish movement in the United States. Notwithstanding attempts to gain subscribers from across the country, there is no doubt that the main centres of Irish population on the east coast dominated. Leading the pack was New York, which raised a whopping $1,453,014—26% of the total. This was followed by $1,037,896 from Massachusetts, and then by California, Illinois and Pennsylvania, which raised $386,941, $381,345 and $540,781 respectively. When measured in per capita terms, Massachusetts was by far the biggest contributor, with $2,692.42 per 10,000 inhabitants. Although the amount of subscribers in a state was highly correlated to the size of the Irish population there, this was not the case for the amount of money subscribed. When measured in terms of the Irish-born population, the state making the largest contribution was Alabama ($18 per Irish person), followed by Oregon ($15), Arizona ($12), Wyoming ($12) and Minnesota ($11). Meanwhile, Massachusetts and New York contributed only $5.66 and $4.75 respectively per Irish-born resident.

Although the British consul general's suspicions about Henry Ford and Standard Oil appear to have been wide of the mark, a number of American industrialists can be identified in the list of subscribers. The largest subscription,

$20,000, came from John McGinley, chairman of the West Penn Steel Company, while Edward L. Doheny, the Californian oil baron and inspiration for the movie *There will be blood*, subscribed $10,000. The vast majority, however, 210,190 of the 276,219 bond certificates sold, were purchased in denominations of just $10. Although these $10 subscriptions contributed just 41% to the total amount raised by the drive, as a demonstration of popular support for Irish independence in America they were invaluable.

The funds raised by the bond drive in the United States were essential in determining the outcome of the Irish War of Independence. Funds remitted from America to Ireland constituted some two-thirds of the Dáil's revenue for the period and, as well as feeding a growing military budget, the bond drive also made possible the establishment of a network of embassies and consulates around the world. Moreover, as a driver and barometer of public opinion in North America, the bond drive was indispensable to the cause of Irish independence. As the Irish Free State Minister of Finance Ernest Blythe remarked in 1923, when proposing the repayment with interest of the bond drive's subscribers, 'If it had not been for the generosity and the faith of the people who subscribed to the Loan there would be no Free State to-day'.

Robin J.C. Adams, an economic historian of the Irish War of Independence, is a research fellow at Queen's University Belfast.

Further reading

M. Carroll, *Money for Ireland: finance, diplomacy, politics, and the first Dáil Éireann loans, 1919–1936* (Westport, CT, 2002).

M. Doorley, *Irish-American diaspora nationalism: the Friends of Irish Freedom, 1916–35* (Dublin, 2005).

D. Lainer-Vos, *Sinews of the nation: constructing Irish and Zionist bonds in the United States* (Cambridge, 2013).

DRESSED TO IMPRESS: THE MATERIAL CULTURE OF THE DÁIL ÉIREANN FOREIGN SERVICE

BY **JOHN GIBNEY**

When the first Dáil established its Ministry of Foreign Affairs in January 1919, it viewed itself as a functioning Irish state in embryo. It was vital to its ambitions and self-image that it deliver this message credibly to outside observers in the hope that they would officially recognise the Dáil government. Consequently, there was an Irish diplomatic service before there was an internationally recognised Irish state. One was meant to lead to the other. The archives of the Dáil's diplomatic service are retained in the National Archives of Ireland, while personal papers held in UCD archives, the National Library of Ireland and the Contemporary Documents collection of the Bureau of Military History in the Irish Military Archives also contain valuable material. Much of this archive has been published by the Royal Irish Academy's Documents on Irish Foreign Policy project. Yet the significance of this documentation lies not just in its contents: the style, too, had a role to play that was intertwined with the substance.

The material culture of the diplomatic service was intended to emphasise the legitimacy of the Dáil's claims by adopting the traditional procedures and etiquette of officialdom, just as any established state's diplomatic service would. There were, of course, limits to this. The Dáil could not realistically act in a way that required formal international recognition by issuing documentation such as passports. And there were also limits to what a government on the run could do. Take, for example, *The Irish Bulletin*, the Dáil's main propaganda publication. By the time the Irish edition ceased publication in December 1921, it was being distributed to as many as 900 recipients in Britain and on the

Continent. Produced in Dublin under extremely difficult circumstances, it was a basic typescript, but the multilingual propaganda printed overseas in Denmark, France, Germany, Italy, Spain and elsewhere was more professionally designed. These publications accounted for a significant portion of expenditure, and they were intended to resemble the official publications that a government might produce. Such material culture subtly reinforced the message that the Dáil was indeed the only legitimate Irish government. The same could be said of ephemera such as business cards and letterheads. It was especially true of the republican bond certificates issued in the United States to raise funds for the Dáil, which were deliberately intended to resemble official currency.

All of these gave a sense of how the Dáil sought to present itself to its intended audiences: as the legitimate government of a formally established Irish Republic. For example, the Dáil's diplomatic service lacked purpose-built physical locations to convey their authority, but there were attempts to overcome this. As the Dáil's representative in Paris, Seán T. Ó Ceallaigh had been based since the previous month in the Grand

Hotel on the Boulevard des Capuchines ('one of the most important', as he put it himself). His early correspondence from Paris used the hotel's own stationery, before he obtained customised notepaper. Ó Ceallaigh also had plans to establish an 'Irish social centre' in Paris, though attempts to link up with the Irish College were unsuccessful. Ó Ceallaigh highlighted the importance of a very different and unofficial material culture in March 1919, when he wrote to Cathal Brugha in Dublin requesting 'a few thousand' for 'smoothing a passage to the presence of the great men here and of securing the ear of the press. *You can get nothing whatsoever done otherwise.*'

Public events also had a role to play in presenting the Irish Republic as a legitimate state, such as the election-style rallies that marked Éamon de Valera's US tour in 1919–20, complete with bands, bunting, flags and ceremonials. The materiality of locations could also be adapted to support the Dáil's diplomatic efforts,

Below: Dressed to impress—George Gavan Duffy with Seán T. Ó Ceallaigh and his wife Cáit in Paris, 1919. Making the case for an Irish republic entailed extensive social engagement. (NLI).

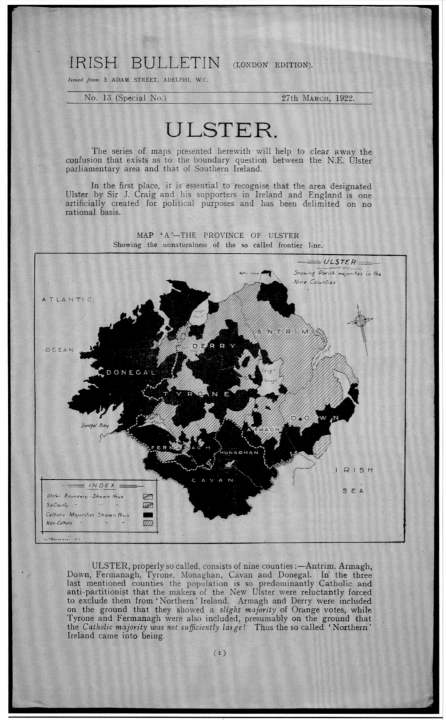

IRISH BULLETIN (LONDON EDITION).

Issued from 3 ADAM STREET, ADELPHI, W.C.

No. 13 (Special No.)   27th MARCH, 1922.

ULSTER.

The series of maps presented herewith will help to clear away the confusion that exists as to the boundary question between the N.E. Ulster parliamentary area and that of Southern Ireland.

In the first place, it is essential to recognise that the area designated Ulster by Sir J. Craig and his supporters in Ireland and England is one artificially created for political purposes and has been delimited on no rational basis.

MAP 'A'—THE PROVINCE OF ULSTER
Showing the unnaturalness of the so called frontier line.

ULSTER, properly so called, consists of nine counties :—Antrim, Armagh, Down, Fermanagh, Tyrone, Monaghan, Cavan and Donegal. In the three last mentioned counties the population is so predominantly Catholic and anti-partitionist that the makers of the New Ulster were reluctantly forced to exclude them from 'Northern' Ireland. Armagh and Derry were included on the ground that they showed a *slight majority* of Orange votes, while Tyrone and Fermanagh were also included, presumably on the ground that the *Catholic majority was not sufficiently large*! Thus the so called 'Northern' Ireland came into being.

(1)

---

although sometimes little effort was required. Writing to Michael Collins from Genoa in May 1921, Donal Hales reported on a visit to Bobbio to attend the ordination of five 'republican' priests during which the 'Sinn Féin' flag was hung from the cathe-

●

Above: 'No rational basis' for partition—a professionally produced version of the *Irish Bulletin* published in London in early 1922 denounces the proposed border. (NLI)

dral, with five more republican banners displayed at the seminary itself. The local bishop had urged his congregation to pray 'for the triumph of Ireland', while Hales noted that 'Columbanus (died 615) has done a lot of propaganda for Ireland in Italy'.

The materials produced by the Dáil's Department of Foreign Affairs demonstrated the Dáil's desire to present itself to the world in a professional manner. Consequently, it

was inevitable that the Department of Foreign Affairs would come to be run along increasingly professional lines, and in February 1921 Robert Brennan became its dedicated 'under-secretary'. In October of that year he argued that Irish representatives being sent abroad needed to be equipped with 'an outfit in accordance with the dignity of the office they are about to fill', and that 'the absolute minimum amount of clothes would consist of dress, morning and lounge suits, a dress hat' (and 'other hats'), along with footwear, a 'good suit case' and a 'dressing case'. The Republic's diplomats were to look the part and, in Brennan's view, £100 would enable each envoy to do so.

Following the Anglo-Irish Treaty, a year later, a more austere approach had crept in. In October 1922 Brennan's successor, Joseph Walshe, informed Count Gerald O'Kelly, the Irish representative in Brussels, that as the Irish Free State came into existence his office was to be downgraded to that of a 'trade agent'. As he would not normally be expected to entertain guests in that capacity, he was ordered to sell off any furniture he had purchased, except for whatever was necessary for a functioning office: 'the work of our trade agents should be done without ostentation of any kind'. The clear implication was that other types of work—such as securing the international recognition of an independent Irish state—*did* require ostentation of some kind.

One might say that the First Dáil's diplomatic service had dressed to impress. Its material culture provides a sidelight on the ambitions and strategies of the Irish independence movement as it navigated the post-war political world.

John Gibney is Department of Foreign Affairs and Trade 100 Project Co-ordinator with the Royal Irish Academy's Documents on Irish Foreign Policy project.

Further reading

M. Kennedy *et al.* (eds), *Documents on Irish Foreign Policy, Vol. 1: 1919–22* (Dublin, 1998).

PROPAGANDA AND PRESS

We were filled with shame that in the name of law and order servants of the British Crown should be guilty of besmirching in the eyes of Ireland the honesty of the British people. The final solution of the Irish problem will not be found in a policy of vengeance. It will have to be found along the lines of conciliation and consent by the more enlightened method of negotiations.

—Report of the (British) Labour Commission to Ireland, January 1921

Image: A similar image of the burning of Cork appeared in the *Illustrated London News* on Saturday 18 December 1920 under the subheading 'DEVASTATION IN THE HEART OF THE CITY AFTER A NIGHT OF FIRE'. British newspapers were reluctant to continue to accept the type of censorship imposed during the Great War. (NLI)

SHREDDING THE PAPER WALL:

REPUBLICAN PROPAGANDA AND INTERNATIONAL PRESS COVERAGE

BY **MAURICE WALSH**

J.G. Farrell's celebrated novel *Troubles*, the first of a trilogy charting the decline of the British Empire, is set in a decaying Anglo-

Irish seaside hotel whose inhabitants are comically detached from the guerrilla warfare raging all around them. Only the central character,

Major Brendan Archer, a shell-shocked veteran of the Great War, keeps up to date with the Irish War of Independence by avidly reading the newspapers. On a visit to Dublin, Major Archer witnesses the assassination of a British intelligence agent in an IRA ambush, but he is not able to grasp his experience until he reads an account of the shooting in the paper next day. 'It was the newspaper which had explained to him what he had seen.'

The major was not alone in relying on the press to find his bearings in a turbulent world. The Irish revolution coincided with the birth of mass democracy in an age when the press was perceived to be a decisive factor shaping the political world. Debates about the influence of newspapers, whether pernicious or uplifting, raged among politicians, intellectuals and journalists in the United States, Britain and the

rest of Europe. Divining the opinions of the newspaper reader was a central concern of politicians and governments eager to mobilise the masses.

This meant that the age of news was also the age of propaganda. From 1914 to 1918 the mainstream press in Britain was co-opted for the war effort. Newspaper proprietors acquiesced in the system of censorship and their journalists felt obliged to comply. Officially approved war correspondents were escorted to the front and their despatches only released once they had been passed by military censors. Over breakfast at Downing Street in December 1917, the Liberal prime minister, David Lloyd George, acknowledged to C.P. Scott, editor of the *Manchester Guardian*, that the true horror of the war was hidden from the public. 'If people really knew [what was going on in the trenches] the war would be stopped tomorrow', Lloyd George admitted. 'But of course, they don't and can't know. The correspondents don't write and the censorship would not pass the truth.'

The success of the British propaganda campaign, acknowledged worldwide, and the enthusiasm shown by newspapers to follow the censorship regime provoked a public debate about the trustworthiness of the press when the war was over. This disillusionment was shared by the correspondents themselves; the memoirs of famous war correspondents were infused with subdued remorse at having betrayed their calling. H.G. Wells summed up a widespread view when he wrote in 1921 that 'there has been a considerable increase of deliberate lying in the British press since 1914, and a

The Road to Peace.
The Cessation of Violence and the Opening up of Negotiations.

The Commission of Inquiry, which visited Ireland on behalf of the British Labour Movement, carried on informal " conversations " with representative leaders of national life with the object of bringing about a cessation of all acts of violence and all provocative acts and the opening up of official negotiations.

The Commission proposed to Cardinal Logue, the Archbishop of Dublin, and representatives of the Executive Committee of the Irish Labour Party and Trade Union Congress, that it should issue an appeal signed by its members and countersigned by representatives of the Irish Labour Movement and by the Irish Catholic Hierarchy.

It was proposed that the appeal should be directed to the British Government and to the recognised leaders of Sinn Fein, urging the cessation of all acts of violence by both sides, in order to produce a period of quiet in Ireland ; that when this unofficial truce had operated for an agreed period, official negotiations should be commenced for an

Official Truce and Agreed Settlement.

The preliminary truce was to be unofficial, and in the nature of an earnest of good intention, but it was to be the first of three related steps to which tentative agreement should be secured in advance from both sides.

This threefold plan was agreed to by the heads of the Roman Catholic Hierarchy and by the representatives of Irish Labour.

The British Government, on the other hand, neither definitely rejected nor actually accepted the proposals. Their attitude was non-committal. They have, however, now resorted to official reprisals.

Hence it is that the reign of violence continues unchecked in Ireland. Neither an unofficial nor an official truce has been arranged. Peace in Ireland and with Ireland remains yet to be established.

THE GOVERNMENT ARE GAMBLING ON A "KNOCK-OUT" BLOW.

LABOUR STANDS FOR RECONCILIATION AND PEACE BY CONSENT.

Printed by the Caledonian Press Ltd. (T.U.), 74 Swinton Street, Gray's Inn Road, W.C. 1—W724 Published by the Labour Party, 33 Eccleston Square, London, S.W. 1. (MM.—26.1.21)

Above right: British Labour outlines 'The Road to Peace'. Press reports played a key role in informing the British public about the reality of the war in Ireland and creating a desire among some for a settlement. (NMI)

Opposite page: A well-armed Auxiliary policeman in Dublin, 1921. Visiting newsmen disliked the 'Auxies' and 'Tans', and reports of their behaviour contributed to turning world opinion against Britain.

marked loss of journalistic self-respect ... a considerable proportion of the [news] is rephrased and mutilated to give a misleading impression to the reader'. When Desmond FitzGerald, the head of the Irish revolutionaries' publicity department, visited London to meet correspondents from foreign newspapers he was struck by how their wartime experience made them wary of anything they construed as propaganda.

The lesson he learned was that

anything that appeared to be propaganda would be treated with suspicion by journalists. So the publicity department's information sheet, the *Irish Bulletin*, went out of its way to appear forensically reliable. It presented incidents from the war in a restrained, pared-back, just-the-facts style, without flourishes, which proclaimed that this was news, not advocacy. Within a few months of its launch, the *Bulletin* was being read by political figures in London and by politicians, diplomats and journalists in Europe and the rest of the world. When correspondents arrived in Ireland, the spokesmen they met—FitzGerald and Erskine Childers—were British-born, urbane and well connected to the media world in London. They in turn opened doors to intellectual apologists for the Sinn Féin cause such as George Russell and the popular historian Alice Stopford Green, whose outlook was essentially the same as that of English liberals. The Sinn Féin spokesmen had established an extraordinary degree of trust with correspondents who came to Ireland. Visiting journalists found the rebels' propaganda operation more alert, more persuasive and more attuned to their needs than the efforts of the government's spokesmen in Dublin Castle. On his return to London in August 1921, a correspondent for *The Times*, Maxwell H.H. MacCartney, wrote an appreciative letter to Desmond FitzGerald: 'I was quite the blue-eyed boy when I got back to the

office and must take this opportunity of thanking you and your office for much of such success as I have apparently managed to score in the eyes of *The Times*'.

Rather than being the singular product of native genius, Sinn Féin's focus on publicity was replicating the practice of other insurgent groups in the new media age. In the early twentieth century, national movements became synonymous with press campaigns in major world cities. Prior to the American intervention in Cuba in 1898, Cuban exiles in New York had helped journalists from the major papers there to write about the scorched-earth tactics being practised by the Spaniards in the effort to suppress Cuban nationalism. Indian nationalists agitated in London and, at the Paris peace conference, every supplicant nation had its publicity agents.

For the Sinn Féin leaders, the presentation of their case for nationhood to the rest of the world was not a sideshow but a central part of their strategy to force the British government to grant Irish independence. The aim was to universalise the Irish experience, inviting visiting journalists to frame their struggle within greater world-historical dimensions. By claiming the right to self-determination, the Irish revolutionaries were aligning themselves with President Woodrow Wilson and connecting the struggle in Ireland with anti-colonial movements around the world who drew inspiration from Wilson's apparent desire to put an end to imperialism. The interest shown in the nationalist cause by the journalists who converged on Ireland to report the war, the commentary and reportage connecting Ireland to world themes, and the prominence given to the Irish struggle in newspapers around the world combined to allow George Gavan Duffy, the first Minister for External Affairs in the new government of the Irish Free State, to boast in a memorandum in 1922 that Ireland was highly regarded around the world because it stood for 'democratic principles, against

Imperialism and upon the side of liberty throughout the world'. This was the master narrative that Sinn Féin pressed on journalists covering the Anglo-Irish war.

While at first many correspondents were prepared to take on trust the official line that the establishment of a parliament in Dublin was a futile piece of political theatre, the tone of the coverage in much of the British press changed as the IRA stepped up its campaign and the authority of the administration in Dublin Castle appeared to crumble. When the Black-and-Tans and the Auxiliaries were introduced in 1920 to bolster the disintegrating RIC, the challenge of controlling perceptions became even more difficult for the British government. Correspondents travelled the country to interview witnesses to police riots, floggings and midnight assassinations. The notorious indiscipline of the Black-and-Tans and Auxiliaries opened a new vista for the reporting from Ireland. They were disliked and shunned by many of the correspondents, who regarded them as neither proper soldiers nor gentlemen.

By contrast, the rebels were widely regarded as legitimate and reliable sources of news. In 1921 the young French journalist Simone Tery travelled from Dublin to County Clare with the IRA commander Michael Brennan. He reminded her, she wrote, of French revolutionaries. 'He looks like a young war god. Whenever he goes down the street, heads turn to admire his vigorous physique, broad shoulders, and perfectly beautiful head.' She described how crowds would follow his car as they passed through villages, boys jumping on the running-board and clinging to the bonnet. She watched twenty IRA Volunteers training in the ruins of a police barracks. 'They acted like a bunch of boys back from a Sunday outing with only the problems of youth.'

As Sinn Féin's public relations campaign blossomed in scale and sophistication, the officials in Dublin Castle appeared more uncertain and increasingly overawed by

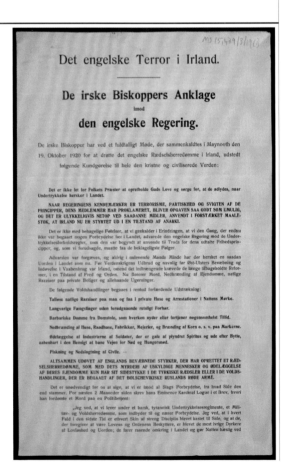

the pace of events. Arthur Griffith had claimed that Britain controlled external views of Ireland, conjuring up the metaphor of the island being surrounded by a paper wall. As the guerrilla campaign progressed, however, the paper wall—if it ever existed—was shredded by visiting correspondents and writers from Europe and the United States who portrayed Ireland as the scene of imperial atrocities. Crucially, British correspondents, stung by criticisms of their submission to wartime censorship in 1914–18, repeatedly challenged their government's presentation of events in Ireland and proclaimed themselves as fearless standard-bearers of truth-telling, reclaiming the idealised role of the press as a watchdog on the powerful. Their critical coverage and the reportage of their international colleagues was seized on by the British government's critics in the House of Commons. 'In France the newspapers are full of Ireland', Captain Anthony Wedgwood Benn told MPs. 'I could quote statements of newspapers of very different opinions all condemning the Irish administration. In Italy every paper is full of news from Ireland, with pictures of the happenings there and accounts of the anarchy and disorder.' He was not wrong; Ireland's troubles were now followed by a global audience. Shortly before the lord mayor of Cork and IRA commandant Terence MacSwiney died in Brixton Prison after 74 days on hunger strike, Marcel Proust dismissed a visitor to his home in Paris who wanted to discuss the latest instalment of *Remembrance of things past*. 'Don't speak to me about De Cote de Guermantes', the great novelist remonstrated with his guest, 'but about the Lord Mayor of Cork, that will be very interesting.'

The former British prime minister Herbert Asquith stressed how the news from Ireland was credible because press reports came not from Sinn Féin but from 'a vast body of absolutely independent, impartial [men], representing the great organs of the Press not only of this country but of America, France and other parts of the civilised world [who] without any prepossession or prejudices were sent there … We have the evidence of these men who have been on the spot, and who are thoroughly qualified by experience, as well as by honesty and judgment, not to distort the facts.'

The British campaign in Ireland was exposed and dissected to a degree that was rarely seen in other imperial small wars in distant colonies. The coverage was uncomfortable for a government sensitive to public opinion and divided about the impact of reprisals on Britain's global reputation. Condemnation of German militarism had been at the core of Allied propaganda during the First World War. In the immediate aftermath of the war, Lloyd George's government advanced legal arguments for prosecuting German war criminals according to British standards of justice. This opened British methods of warfare to scrutiny and challenge; the campaign to subdue the Irish revolutionaries became a highly visible test of some of the most cherished imperial illusions.

During the Victorian era foreign correspondents from the major powers were generally reliable imperialists, willing bearers of the 'white man's burden'. In the Wilsonian era, however, imperialism and militarism were no longer fashionable, and correspondents were as likely to be sympathetic to national and cultural diversity as they were to be unreconstructed chauvinists. Repeatedly correspondents argued that the methods employed by the Black-and-Tans undermined Britain's post-war standing, as—in the words of *The Times*—'the proved champion of civilisation'. International press coverage spread the notoriety of the war of reprisals in Ireland around the globe; descriptions of a British *freikorps* who self-consciously modelled themselves on the gunslingers of the Wild West were little aid to the image that the British government was trying to project to the world. The British writer J.L. Hammond quoted approvingly the assessment of a French journalist

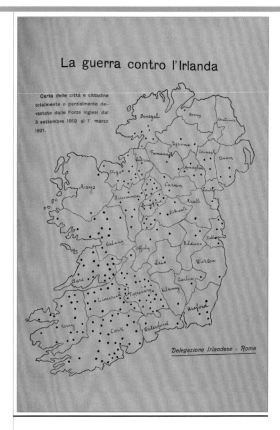

La guerra contro l'Irlanda

who said that 'the British government was trying to subdue a people as intelligent as any in Europe by the means that European governments use for the correction of Berbers'.

Maurice Walsh teaches history at Goldsmiths, University of London.

Further reading

O. O'Hanlon, 'Press coverage from abroad', in J. Crowley, D. Ó Drisceoil & M. Murphy (eds), *Atlas of the Irish Revolution* (Cork, 2017).

M. Walsh, *The news from Ireland: foreign correspondents and the Irish Revolution* (London, 2008).

M. Walsh, *Bitter freedom: Ireland in a revolutionary world 1918–23* (London, 2015).

● Above: 'La guerra contro l'Irlanda'—a map showing British reprisals in Ireland produced by republican diplomats in Rome. (NLI)

● Opposite page: 'Det engelske Terror i Irland'—Irish diplomatic newsletter for a Danish audience denounces British terror. Irish propaganda material was professionally produced and was usually regarded as accurate by international audiences. (NLI)

THE NEWS OF THE WORLD:

A GLOBAL READING OF THE FIRST DÁIL

BY **DARRAGH GANNON**

On 21 January 1919, Dáil Éireann addressed the international community for the first time. On that date Irish republicans arrived at the Mansion House, Dublin, intent on establishing a 'successor state' in waiting. They would face significant challenges in translating the first meeting of Dáil Éireann into a story for international newspapers.

Of the 101 MPs elected in Ireland at the United Kingdom general election in December 1918, 29 took their seats on 21 January 1919. Standing before an expectant audience of 1,000—among them some 70 foreign news reporters—they presented themselves as 'Teachtaí Dála' ('Deputies of the Dáil').

Speaking in Irish, Cathal Brugha, then acting prime minister, proclaimed the legislative powers of the revolutionary assembly, constituting the Dáil ministries of Finance, Foreign Affairs, Home Affairs and Defence. Brugha announced the 'Declaration of Independence', ratifying the Irish Republic proclaimed in arms in 1916; English and French translations followed.

The 'Message to the Free Nations of the World', read by Count Plunkett in French (and by J.J. O'Kelly in Irish), made the case for international recognition of the Irish Republic 'at the dawn of the promised era of self-determination'. Plunkett, alongside the imprisoned Arthur Griffith and Éamon de Valera, was delegated to address the Paris peace conference. The 'Democratic Programme', Dáil Éireann's blueprint for social reform, was recited in Irish and English. Concluding at 5.20pm, the first Dáil could be read as the government of Ireland established.

Reports of Dáil Éireann circulated widely across Europe via press correspondents, agencies and other international communication networks. The London dailies, in their coverage of this historic event, remarked upon the impracticality of Sinn Féin self-government: 'the country has arrived at a political cul-de-sac where the nominal leaders can neither retreat nor advance' (*Daily Mail*). The left-wing *Daily Herald*, alone, struck a discordant note: 'a good beginning is half the work'. The opening of a Dublin parliament, the press summarised, was an illogical political act. The reading of speeches *as Gaeilge* accounted for the limited reporting of the Dáil's proceedings in the British press. Only *The Times* chronicled the day's events and discussion in any detail.

Reflecting on Britain's influence over the international press and representations of Ireland to the world, Arthur Griffith once famously used the metaphor of a 'paper wall'. It formed a barrier that republicans struggled to break through: writing from London as late as 1921, Dáil Éireann envoy Art O'Brien would comment that 'our people here do not yet envisage the orders of An Dáil as positive and definite'.

In January 1919, the news from Paris *was* the news of the world. Opening the pages of the French press thus opens 'Dáil Éireann' to transnational translation. Taking their copy from the French news agency Havas, for example, both *Le Matin* and *L'Intransigeant* carried brief pieces on Dáil Éireann's three founding documents without comment. Written off the front page, 'le parlement sinn-fein' read not as part of the 'new world order' at Versailles but as part of the new world disorder beyond it. 'The French press has been most timid about touching the Irish Question', Seán T. O'Kelly wrote exasperatedly to de Valera, following his appointment as Dáil Éireann envoy to Paris in February 1919; 'you have no idea of the difficulty of the French papers and the delicate handling they require'.

If Parisian newspapers published a French version of 'Dáil Éireann', the Russian press reported a different story. Indeed, the Soviet party's national daily, *Pravda* (*Truth*), took little interest in the first meeting of Dáil Éireann. Events in Dublin, when published, were reported as an international curiosity, external to the interests of the Soviet regime and its readers. Writing to Dublin from Russia in 1921, the Dáil's envoy to Moscow, Patrick MacCartan, noted the limited impact of news of Ireland's revolution in the Soviet Union:

'… the newspapers printed in Russian on the whole I believe are almost entirely propaganda intended for the Russian people … the whole aim is to propagate the ideals of Communism and very little attention is given to any movement in any country which does not tend to that direction … the revolution in Ireland was a national one and hence it was concluded had little or nothing in common with Communism or the "world revolution".'

Reports of an Irish parliament were communicated from Europe to North America. A feature of the American coverage was how its reporting of the Dáil's 'Address to the Free Nations of the World' centred on Ireland's claims to global importance. American press reports also suggested historical parallels between the Irish and American founding documents: 'Sinn Feiners' Bill of Independence', was how the *Chicago Tribune* described it.

American interpretations of events in Dublin, however, were not replicated across the border in Canada. While the Toronto-based national daily, *The Globe*, published Associated Press content, it adopted an imperial position, in line with the language from London: 'they call themselves a parliament … the Dublin performance will be a boon to the tail-twisting elements in the United States and the British Empire'. 'Never forget', de Valera would wire to Dublin from New York in 1920, 'that the press is an instrument used by the enemy.'

News of 'Dáil Éireann' crossed the Latin language barrier, with reports of the 'Irish Republic' reaching Argentina, Brazil and Chile. Their press offered an alternative South American perspective. The establishment of a parliament in Dublin was reported as part of the 'greater war' story on continental Europe. Dáil Éireann would appoint envoys to Argentina, Brazil and Chile in 1921. 'Until real progress is made in diplomatic and trade relations with Argentina, Chile and Brazil', its Buenos Aires representative, Patrick Little, would later remark, 'there is no use wasting money on the other republics—except on press propaganda.'

Reports of Ireland spread further afield, reaching English-speaking newspapers in Ghana, Nigeria, Sierra Leone, Uganda and modern-day Zimbabwe via Reuters, that key 'information broker' of the British Empire, but it was in relation

VOL. XIV. NO. 21.
JANUARY 19, 1922

MID-WEEK PICTORIAL

PRICE TEN CENTS
(CANADA 15 CENTS)

AN ILLUSTRATED WEEKLY PUBLISHED BY The New York Times COMPANY

ARTHUR GRIFFITH
Head of the Irish Free State.

to South Africa, especially, that news of the Dáil prompted greatest concern. 'The republican campaign may have more far-reaching consequences than we have yet imagined', Johannesburg's *International* newspaper judged; 'its effect on the revolutionary movement in South Africa needs to be taken into account.' Arriving on the Cape as Dáil envoy in 1921, P.J. Little would remind the cabinet in Dublin that 'the English speaking community is not interested, part of it [is] intensely anti-Irish and anti-Catholic … the English papers are entirely jingo'.

●

Above: Arthur Griffith—claimed that Britain controlled external views of Ireland, conjuring up the metaphor of the island being surrounded by a 'paper wall'. (*New York Times' Mid-Week Pictorial*, vol. XIV, no. 21, 19 January 1922)

Irish representatives would find it difficult to get a fair press for Dáil Éireann in British-controlled Africa.

News of an Irish parliament made waves across the Indian Ocean, reaching the English-speaking press in modern-day Bangladesh and Pakistan, in addition to India. Reuters' cables, for example, carried news from London to Mumbai—'Sinn Fein assembly, independence declared' (*Times of India*)—and Lahore: 'here is a Reuters telegram: the Sinn Fein Parliament, in a secret session, appointed a Premier and four Ministers' (*The Tribune*).

Further east, London news networks linked metropolitan Asia. Port cities along the South China Sea exchanged information in English as part of their global trade. Leaders in the *Canton Times*, *Shanghai Times* and the Hong Kong-based *South China Morning Post*, accordingly, précised the 'Irish Republic' in columns of news from London. British influence, indeed, extended across the East China Sea to Tokyo, where the independently owned *Japan Times* carried the London *Times*' news reports of the Dáil's first meeting in January 1919: 'Demand English leave Ireland'. Dáil Éireann would

begin translating its documents into Mandarin and Japanese, for export, from January 1921.

The press in Australia and New Zealand also imported news of Ireland directly from London. The *Times*' reports of Dáil Éireann, for example, were carried in many newspapers. These accounts, however, were far from a London press writ large. Reports of Dáil Éireann were subtly re-edited in the pages of the Australasian press to equate Irish self-government with violence and disloyalty. Some opinion pieces, as in the Melbourne *Argus*, were more explicitly hostile to Irish republican aspirations: 'Trouble will come out of the irregular assembly of Dublin'. The Dáil Éireann envoy to Australia and New Zealand, Ormonde Grattan Esmonde, would report to Dublin in 1921 that 'republicanism and separatism ... are now enthusiastically suppressed as "sedition" and "treason"'.

Proclaiming an independent Irish parliament, and Irish Republic, as established fact, the Mansion House assembly issued a recognisable message to the 'free nations of the world'. The First Dáil was a

global event, narrated by newspapers around the world according to language, political culture and international exchange.

Darragh Gannon is a research fellow at Queen's University Belfast, where he is working on the UK Arts and Humanities Research Council-funded project A Global History of Irish Revolution, 1916–23.

Further reading

A. Mitchell, *Revolutionary government in Ireland: Dáil Éireann, 1919–22* (Dublin, 1995).

S. Potter, *News and the British world: the emergence of an imperial press system, 1876–1922* (Oxford, 2003).

Top: *Le Petit Journal*, 23 January 1919—Seán T. O'Kelly complained that 'the French press has been most timid about touching the Irish Question ... you have no idea of the difficulty of the French papers and the delicate handling they require'.

Above: *Japan Times & Mail*, 25 January 1919—news of the First Dáil, reprinted from the London *Times*, was carried by the press in Asia. By 1921 Dáil reports were being translated into Mandarin and Japanese.

'TELLING THE TRUTH AND NOTHING BUT THE TRUTH ABOUT IRELAND':

HANNA SHEEHY SKEFFINGTON AND THE PROPAGANDA WAR IN AMERICA 1917–18

BY **MARGARET WARD**

I n the post-Rising period the priority for Irish republicans was to tell the world that an Irish republic had been established for six days over Easter 1916 in Dublin. No one knew when the Great War would come to an end, but the objective was to ensure that Ireland's case to be treated as a small nation would be included in any peace negotiations. With turmoil in Europe and a large Irish-American community ready to embrace the republican cause, the United States was the obvious destination. It was where Hanna Sheehy Skeffington decided to travel, her objective being to recount the tragedy of her husband Frank, journalist and pacifist, brutally shot in Portobello Barracks during the Rising. Despite securing a Commission of Inquiry under Sir John Simon, Hanna was incensed by Britain's refusal to acknowledge all the events related to Captain Bowen-Colthurst's reign of terror on the Dublin streets, and she declared her determination to 'tell the truth and nothing but the truth about Ireland, Great Britain and the War'.

Denied a passport by the British, Hanna travelled with her son Owen using a false identity, posing as 'Mrs Mary Gribbin'. Although initially treated by many Americans as simply an innocent widow of the conflict, Hanna made it clear that she had a strong political motive in coming to tell her story. She hated what she called the 'sob stories' in the press and the endless photos taken of herself and Owen. In references to the death of Frank in her speeches, she made it clear that 'It would be a poor tribute to my husband if grief were to break my spirit. It shall not do so. I am not here just to harrow your hearts by a passing thrill, to

Above: President Woodrow Wilson—Sheehy Skeffington secured an audience with the president, who she claimed received her courteously and 'acknowledged smilingly his Irish blood'.

Left: Hanna Sheehy Skeffington—she travelled to the United States during 1917 under an alias, with the objective of exposing the truth behind the brutal murder of her husband.

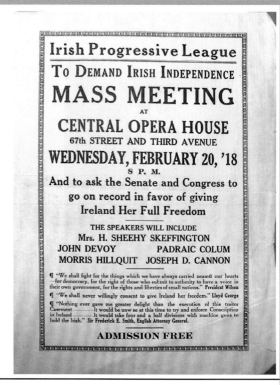

Irish Progressive League
To Demand Irish Independence
MASS MEETING
AT
CENTRAL OPERA HOUSE
67th STREET AND THIRD AVENUE
WEDNESDAY, FEBRUARY 20, '18
8 P. M.
And to ask the Senate and Congress to
go on record in favor of giving
Ireland Her Full Freedom

THE SPEAKERS WILL INCLUDE
Mrs. H. SHEEHY SKEFFINGTON
JOHN DEVOY   PADRAIC COLUM
MORRIS HILLQUIT   JOSEPH D. CANNON

❡ "We shall fight for the things which we have always carried nearest our hearts—for democracy, for the right of those who submit to authority to have a voice in their own government, for the rights and liberties of small nations." President Wilson
❡ "We shall never willingly consent to give Ireland her freedom." Lloyd George
❡ "Nothing ever gave me greater delight than the execution of this traitor Casement .... It would be unwise at this time to try and enforce Conscription in Ireland .... it would take four and a half divisions with machine guns to hold the Irish." Sir Frederick E. Smith, English Attorney General.

ADMISSION FREE

Above: On her US tour Sheehy Skeffington shared platforms with both Irish and American radicals, speaking in New York with the veteran Fenian John Devoy, socialist Morris Hillquit and union leader Joseph D. Cannon. (NLI)

feed you on horrors for sensation's sake.' She was an experienced political activist, a militant campaigner for the vote and a woman used to meetings with politicians both in Ireland and Westminster. Of all the political refugees from Ireland that were in the United States at this time, Hanna Sheehy Skeffington was the one with the most experience and confidence in lobbying. In his biography of Liam Mellows, Desmond Greaves describes her as a 'fearless, tireless and inspired propagandist'. In the first days after her arrival in America she met with former President Roosevelt and also Colonel House, a close confidant of President Woodrow Wilson, informing them 'of the terrible Portobello murders, of the court-martial, the shielding of the guilty parties, of the shooting of James Connolly'.

The lecture she delivered was entitled 'British militarism as I have known it'. This was turned into a pamphlet, banned in England and Ireland during the war but with a wide circulation through Canada, South America and Australia. After the United States entered the war in April 1917 her talk became 'What does Ireland want?'. Another pamphlet, *Impressions of Sinn Fein in America*, not published until 1919 owing to wartime censorship, provided vivid accounts of her experiences and the fevered atmosphere within American political circles as the country entered the war on the British side.

While Hanna asserted that her lecture was confined 'entirely to facts without personal comment' as she dealt with 'the horrors that have become the platitudes and the every-day happenings in a country under military occupation', in reality she provided more than mere facts, given her own position as someone who had participated in the Rising through carrying supplies and messages from the GPO to the College of Surgeons. She told her audiences: 'I knew the Irish Republican leaders, and am proud to call Connolly, Pearse, M[a]cDonagh, Plunkett, O'Rahilly and others friends—proud to have known them and had their friendship. They fought a clean fight against terrible odds—and terrible was the price they had to pay. They were filled with a high idealism.' James Connolly had told her that the Proclamation would grant equality to women, and in all her speeches she emphasised that the Proclamation 'gave equal citizenship to women, beating all records, except that of the Russian Revolutionists, and their Revolution came later'. Her pamphlet and speeches provided a concise and clear statement of what the Irish and Irish-Americans were asking of the United States regarding the future of Ireland:

'... our small nation, Ireland, has a right also to its place in the sun. We look to the United States particularly to help us in this matter. The question of Ireland is not, as suggested by England, "A domestic matter". It is an international one, just as the case of Belgium, Serbia and other small nationalities is. We want our case to come up at the Peace Conference ...'

Tasked with investigating Hanna, the Bureau of Investigation at the US Department of Justice concluded that her lectures were 'extremely pro-Irish and anti-British but that they do not attack the United States'. Significantly, however, her husband Frank was now described by agents as 'an Irish traitor', or as a revolutionary executed for his part in the Rising. The military intelligence section of the War Department sent agents to a wide number of meetings that she addressed. Agent Swift reported her speech in San Antonio in October 1917:

'The lady, who is highly educated, delivered a very interesting lecture showing why Ireland should be considered at the peace conference at the end of the war ... Her remarks could not be construed anyway as anti-American or anti-ally as she is quite well instructed as to her rights in speech from all appearances.'

As a university graduate in French and German, and a frequent traveller to Europe, Hanna's personal preference was for a future in which European countries would be closely aligned—an alignment in which Ireland would play its full part:

'At the end of the war we hope to see a "United Europe" on the model of your own United States, where each state is free and independent, yet all are part of a great federation. We want Ireland to belong to this united Europe, and not to be a vassal of Great Britain, a province of the British Empire, governed without consent.'

Mixing in circles much wider than the socially conservative Irish-American community, Hanna was invited to be a member of the

Heterodoxy Club in Greenwich Village, formed by women who relished their non-conformity to convention, many of whom were lesbians and advocated extremely radical politics. Elizabeth Gurley Flynn, the 'rebel girl', was a member, as were many other socialist and feminist women. She was also a friend of the suffragist Alice Park, who had visited Ireland in 1910 after attending a suffrage congress in Europe. Park, from Palo Alto, now worked for Congressman John Raker of California, who chaired the House Committee on Woman Suffrage. Female suffrage in America, as in Ireland and Britain, remained a live issue.

The activities of the two women are recorded in reports by Seamus O'Sheel, appointed by John Devoy to help Hanna with her introductions to politicians on Capitol Hill—but also to report back to Devoy on Hanna's actions. O'Sheel's acerbic description of Park made his hostility to feminists evident: 'The latter is a suffragist, pacifist, vegetarian, prohibitionist, anti-tobacooist and professional writer, and looks all those things'.

His reports portray Hanna as a self-confident woman, well able to organise her own introductions, as she brushed aside his contacts as 'small fry' and 'old Tammanyites'. On her first visit to Capitol Hill, on 8 January 1918, O'Sheel reported that, as the British ambassador walked past her, 'Mrs Skeffington decided to approach him right then

●

Below: Irish-American women protest in Washington DC, 1920—women played a major role in the agitation that developed in the United States during the War of Independence.

Mrs. Sheehy - Skeffington

WILL SPEAK

TUESDAY, APRIL 16th

AT THE

MASS MEETING

TO BE HELD AT THE

CIVIC CENTER AUDITORIUM

TO HELP SECURE

Tom Mooney a New Trial

The Irish World has been a bulwark for Justice in these cases. It has prevailed on Mrs. Skeffington to add her powerful voice to that of President Wilson to secure Justice for Tom Mooney and Warren K. Billings

Under Auspices of MACHINISTS UNION LODGE No. 68
Indorsed by San Francisco Labor Council and Affiliated Bodies

... she chatted with Spring-Rice ten minutes and made appointment for the Embassy at 3 pm'.

Washington was particularly hectic, as a backlog of legislation—held up while a special War Congress had been called to discuss the war—was going before Congress. A vote on the 19th amendment to the Constitution, giving women the right to vote, was debated on 10 January, where it passed by a two-thirds majority. Hanna joined in the celebrations and had meetings with Jeanette Rankin from Montana (the first woman to be elected to Congress) and other politicians. She hoped that Rankin could persuade the House of Representatives to

● Above: In San Francisco Sheehy Skeffington spoke in support of labour activist Tom Mooney, who faced a death sentence on trumped-up charges.

support a resolution that Ireland was amongst the small nations for whose independence the United States was fighting. O'Sheel admitted to Devoy that Senator la Follette was 'much impressed' with Mrs Skeffington. That day also saw Hanna achieve her biggest success—an interview with President Wilson.

A message had been smuggled to her, stating that the accompanying petition had to be delivered to the president personally. This had been signed by prominent Irish women—Constance Markievicz, Jennie Wyse Power, Louise Gavan Duffy, Áine Ceannt, Kathleen Clarke, Grace Gifford and others—putting forward the claim of Ireland for self-determination and appealing to President Wilson to include Ireland among the small nations for whose freedom the United States was fighting. Bainbridge Colby, who

had chaired Hanna's first meeting in Carnegie Hall in January 1917, was now a secretary of state in Wilson's cabinet and he facilitated the meeting. Hanna said of the occasion, 'I was the first Irish exile and the first Sinn Féiner to enter the White House and the first to wear there the badge of the Irish Republic, which I took care to pin in my coat before I went'.

At Cumann na mBan's 1918 Convention, the organisation paid tribute to Mrs Sheehy Skeffington as a woman 'to whom we owe a great deal, as her persistence and courage wore down the efforts of English diplomacy to prevent her reaching the President'. In describing the event to Devoy, Hanna sent a copy of the women's petition and said that the president 'was personally very courteous and acknowledged smilingly his Irish blood'. Another prominent person who gave her an interview was the industrialist Henry Ford, a political supporter of Wilson who was, she said, in favour of an Irish Republic and very dismissive of 'British greatness'. Ford believed that they would soon 'get more democracy than they bargain for'.

During the course of speaking at more than 250 meetings in 21 states, Hanna involved herself with other political causes, perhaps most notably that of labour activist Tom Mooney, then under sentence of death on a trumped-up charge intended to discredit the Industrial Workers of the World union. When she first visited San Francisco she attended the trial of Mooney's wife Rena and, following a request from Mooney's mother (an emigrant from County Mayo), visited Tom in jail. Mooney was eventually to serve 23 years in jail, despite even President Wilson acknowledging his innocence. When Hanna returned west in 1918 she spoke on Mooney's behalf on 16 April at a meeting sponsored by the radical *Irish World* newspaper and endorsed by the labour council and trade unions. The platform included Rena Mooney and the Cork-born labour activist Mother Jones. Mother Jones urged the government not to bomb Germany because that would be to bomb the large working class in that country.

Hanna's association with such remarks, in the context of war hysteria, appears to have led to increased opposition at further events. She succeeded in speaking at the Dreamland Rink on 17 April, one of the largest halls in America, but concerted efforts were made to prevent her from speaking at other events. Under pressure from the San Francisco office of the Department of Justice (which reported that her remarks were 'calculated to discourage enlistments and particularly encourage women not to support war measures'), the management of the Dreamland Rink cancelled a further meeting on 24 April. She and her supporters marched through the streets to the Red Branch Hall,

with Hanna declaring that she had not 'the slightest intention to allow myself to be muzzled'. When she and the Revd William Short, the meeting's chairman (and 'a rank socialist', according to the Department of Justice), were brought to a police station for questioning, Hanna declared that she would hunger strike. A telegram in her support was sent to the White House and the case against her was dismissed. Short was released on bail while a case against him on charges of violating the Espionage Act was prepared for Grand Jury hearing.

Her last meeting, in Madison Square Garden, New York, on 4 May 1918, was organised by the Irish Progressive League. She told her audience that she felt she had spoken so often that she would prefer to go home and keep Ireland safe from conscription and safe for democracy. Each word and cheer in her speech was noted by a Secret Service agent. Her tone was much less measured than it had been previously:

'And it seems to me if it is to be decided in this country that it is treason to the United States to talk against conscription in Ireland then I think the best place for any self-respecting man or woman is prison (wild applause) … I say, if the continuance of the British Empire depends upon the life of a

single Irish conscript, then I say, let the British Empire be wiped out … I for one will lose no sleep at any time over the extinction of the British Empire (wild applause).'

The British ambassador wanted her to be sent home as a 'dangerous agitator'. She, too, wanted to leave. On 27 June 1918 Hanna and her son Owen were permitted to leave America, travelling back with Nora Connolly and Margaret Skinnider. In those eighteen months she had made a personal journey from feminist activist, anti-war campaigner and bereaved widow to that of declared Sinn Féiner.

Margaret Ward is Visiting Research Fellow in History at Queen's University, Belfast. With thanks to Micheline Sheehy Skeffington for additional information on Hanna's tour.

Further reading

D. Greaves, *Liam Mellows and the Irish Revolution* (London, 1971).

M. Ward, *Hanna Sheehy Skeffington: a life* (Cork, 1997).

M. Ward (ed.), *Hanna Sheehy Skeffington, suffragette and Sinn Féiner: her memoirs and political writings* (Dublin, 2017).

Above: 'Independence Day'—Irish-American women protest in Roxbury, Mass., 4 July 1920. (Bureau of Military History)

DIASPORAS

Suppose the aborigines claimed to be entitled to conduct the government of Australia as the sole original owners. Would we for a moment submit to a debate on the subject? Yet that is what we are asked to do now.

—Loyalist demonstration, Melbourne; quoted in *The Vigilant*, the official organ of the Victorian Protestant Federation, 17 March 1921

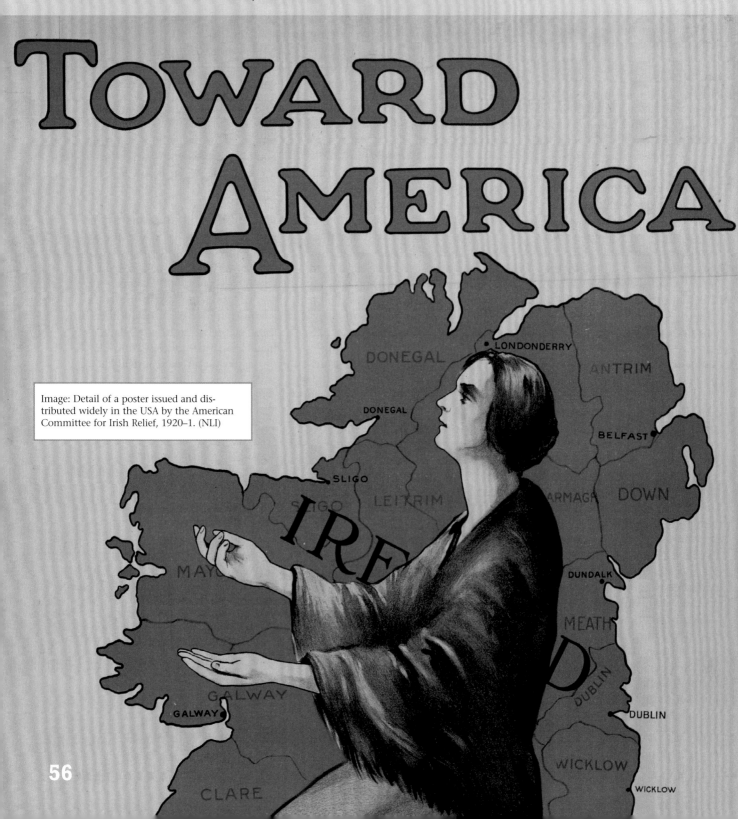

TOWARD AMERICA

Image: Detail of a poster issued and distributed widely in the USA by the American Committee for Irish Relief, 1920–1. (NLI)

'PENNILESS REFUGEES':

THE PLIGHT OF SOUTHERN IRISH LOYALISTS ABROAD

BY **BRIAN HUGHES**

At a meeting hosted in the Mansion House in London in June 1923, the duke of Northumberland—a fiery, die-hard Conservative—urged his audience to 'fulfil an obligation and to discharge a duty to certain people whom you and I owe a very deep debt of gratitude, but whom you and I have sacrificed for the sake of our own peace and quiet'. That obligation was due to the loyalists of 'southern' (26-county) Ireland, who had found themselves on the losing side of the settlement that partitioned the island and created the Irish Free State. Sir Edward Carson, doyen of Ulster unionism but Dublin-born, followed Northumberland to the platform. Carson offered an admission that 'it was only right that he should plead the cause of the Southern Loyalist, because he was a false teacher from his youth up'. Had they not heeded his advice to 'trust in the intelligence, and the fairness of the English character', and were instead 'party to murder and assassination, arson, pillage, and rape', they would now 'be welcomed in Downing Street', as republicans had seemingly been. Convictions held among the loyalists of the 'lost' counties of Ulster—Cavan, Donegal and Monaghan—that it was Carson and his followers who had first abandoned their southern brethren were quietly ignored.

The cartoonist Ernest Forbes (working as 'Shemus') was one who picked up on the potential contradiction. Days after Carson's Mansion House speech, a Shemus cartoon appeared in *The Freeman's Journal* under the title 'Ulster Will Fight, etc.'. In the cartoon, Carson speaks to a group of upright, if elderly and threadbare, gentlemen:

> CARSON TO SOUTHERN UNIONIST EXILES—"I'm sorry I ever told you to trust England!"

Above left: Alan Ian Percy, 8th duke of Northumberland, chairman of the Southern Irish Loyalists Relief Association—one of many British conservative 'die-hards' who were despondent at the loss of southern Ireland. (NPG)

ULSTER WILL FIGHT, ETC.

CARSON TO SOUTHERN UNIONIST EXILES—"I'm sorry I ever told you to trust England!"

SOUTHERN UNIONIST CHORUS—"We're sorry you ever told us to trust Ulster!"

SOUTHERN UNIONIST
CHORUS—"We're sorry you ever told us to trust Ulster!"

The cartoon is a clever critique of the use by Carson, Northumberland and others of southern Irish loyalists for immediate political purposes—in this case to denigrate David Lloyd George's coalition government of

● Above: 'We're sorry you ever told us to trust Ulster!'—a 'Shemus' cartoon in the *Freeman's Journal* casts a cold eye on Ulster unionists' abandonment of their southern brethren.

● Opposite page: The Beltons, William, Charles and Henry, in the uniform of the Palestine Police Force, *c.* 1920s. The three brothers from Leitrim had previously served in the RIC. (Belton family)

1919–22. The rhetoric that inspired Forbes demonstrates that the 'Irish question' retained its potency in British politics after 1921.

Forbes's use of the word 'exiles' touches on another aspect of Irish revolutionary history that has drawn much attention (if not consensus) from historians: the reasons for the significant decline (about a third) of the non-Catholic population of the 26 counties between 1911 and 1926. 'Ulster Will Fight, etc.' subtly references this 'exodus', while also playing up to stereotypes of the southern Irish loyalist as a member of the declining landlord class. Loyalist migration was, of course, more complex than that, also encompassing middle- and working-class Protestants. A significant number of

Catholics also fitted into a broader—though perhaps additionally complex—category of loyalist, including ex-soldiers, ex-policemen and their families. Southern Irish loyalists were repeatedly described by British and Northern (though not, of course, Free State) governments as 'exiles' and 'refugees'. Whether or not this designation was accurate, the impact and potential political potency of these labels is important.

Advocates like Carson and the duke of Northumberland (who, incidentally, had no direct connection to Ireland) had access to the right-wing national press in Britain, where they published appeals, articles, letters and reports. This was often under the auspices of the Southern Irish Loyalists Relief Association (SILRA), chaired by Northumberland. The majority of loyalist migrants had gone to Britain, the primary destination for all Irish migration in this period. Even aside from physical movement, however, this 'exodus'—real, perceived or otherwise—had far wider resonance. The same depictions of persecution, suffering and want delivered to audiences in Britain were also communicated to readers in the Dominions. In April 1923, for instance, the vice-chairman of SILRA, I.W. Raymond, wrote to *The Argus* in Melbourne to 'elicit the sympathy' of its readers 'for the loyalists of Southern Ireland who have endured many grievous wrongs and are now in dire distress and affliction'. Following a graphic depiction of the circumstances of 'penniless refugees', Raymond suggested that SILRA 'could appeal to no more sympathetic people than its fellow Dominion compatriots'.

Like nationalists and republicans, those lobbying on behalf of southern Irish loyalists saw rhetorical value in placing the so-called 'plight' of Irish loyalists in a global context. Conservative MP Sir William Davison, for example, suggested that 'If the King's loyal subjects who had been driven from their homes had been Belgian or Greek refugees, large sums would have been placed at their disposal, but unfortunately they are only British subjects who are suffering because of their loyalty to the King'. The idea that these were loyal citizens of the Union and the Empire cruelly betrayed and abandoned by the British government's willing surrender to republicans in 1921 was a recurring theme. This was rhetoric that had political value for the die-hard right in Britain, but also for loyalists and conservatives across the empire.

The Watchman, the organ of the Australian Protestant Defence Association and published in Sydney, mirrored Davison's suggestion that Irish loyalists were being unfairly ignored. It complained of 'the obtrusive sympathy which we are displaying for those who suffer in Russia and elsewhere. All the world over we hear of funds collected to save the children, to feed the starving, to shelter the refugees. Our first duty is to our own fellows.' An 'Irish Loyalist Immigration Committee' was thus being formed in Sydney 'with the object of redeeming these unfortunate people'. The Australian mainstream press also reproduced material published in British newspapers. In May 1922, for instance, a *Daily Express* article by Carson pleading the case of Irish loyalists 'desperately clinging to the hope that they will be succoured by the great Empire'—and unfavourably comparing the neglect of Irish loyalists with British support for the 'Jewish State of Palestine'—was widely carried in Australian newspapers.

Such propaganda, by its nature, generalises and exaggerates. The narratives of loyalist emigrants themselves, meanwhile, reveal greater nuance and complexity. The Irish-born members of the disbanded Royal Irish Constabulary (RIC) are an illustrative example. While it is impossible to get accurate figures, after the force was wound up in 1922 up to 2,000 disbanded policemen left Ireland, of about 13,000 in total. The majority, therefore, remained at home, but the historical narrative is potentially skewed by the dominance of surviving accounts by those who labelled themselves as victims, complained or sought redress. Moreover, many Catholic

policemen would not have considered themselves loyalist at all, although some did explicitly define themselves in that way when applying for compensation to the Irish Grants Committee. But for the southern loyalist lobby at least, ex-policemen (and ex-servicemen) formed a homogeneous and unproblematic cohort of loyalist 'refugees'.

The majority of those who left Ireland went to Britain; among a sample of 366 RIC pensioners to collect payments outside the Irish Free State after 1922 only twenty went further afield. Even this essentially remained imperial migration: seven were in Canada, four in Australia and one in the United States, while eight collected pensions in Palestine. More than 250 Irish-born ex-RIC joined the Palestinian gendarmerie in the 1920s, while others joined colonial forces elsewhere. This was often necessary to continue a career in policing outside Ireland, with limited opportunities available in Britain. The chief of the London Metropolitan Police was not keen on Irish-born men with expensive pensionable experience and 'preconceived ideas of Police service', especially

the type seen in Ireland, 'which', he asserted, 'was more of a military nature than that of a civilian Police force'.

Three of the four Belton brothers of a Carrick-on-Shannon Church of Ireland family joined the Palestinian gendarmerie in the 1920s, living away from Ireland for the rest of their lives, along with two surviving sisters. Charles Belton, the youngest, went to New Zealand after Palestine to continue his police career, later working as a land agent, serving as president of the New Zealand Chess Association and standing unsuccessfully as mayor of Auckland in 1944. William Sidley had an equally unique career. Having gone first to his wife's native Belfast after disbandment, Sidley accepted a position as depot inspector in the Jamaica Constabulary and moved his family there in December 1922. Clearly over-qualified for the role, Sidley quickly rose to be deputy inspector-general of the force. When he died in 1944, an obituary in the *Kingston Observer* noted that he was 'considered one of the most efficient and popular officers that had ever come from abroad'.

colony' in Hertfordshire. A *Daily Mail* report offered a poignant but optimistic view of their existence there. 'It was strange to meet these fine, perfectly disciplined men as refugees in a pretty English village', the correspondent wrote:

> 'The men are living primarily on their pensions ... but they are all anxious to find work ... and these splendid men, remarkable for their physique and intelligence, are being wasted. Their wives are delighted with the picturesque, well-built houses found for them ... The women are very brave. The horrors and fears of the last five years are seen in their haunted eyes, but they seek to forget their sufferings in the pride of their pretty homes. The children, with the adaptability of youth, are already perfectly at home.'

An RIC tribunal was formed to administer and distribute the grants, allowances and other financial arrangements afforded to disbanded men. In 1924 the tribunal reported that facilitating men to travel to Australia, Canada and New Zealand had generally been a success; a smaller number had gone to South Africa, but this was not recommended unless the applicant had a 'knowledge of farming and can raise at least £1,000 in capital'. Disbanded policemen were in a more advantageous position than other settlers, as they had access to additional capital from commuted pensions and direct access to the Dominions Office through RIC resettlement branches. The tribunal expressed a preference for emigration within the empire (with 'their capital applied productively' there) but did not object when an applicant had reason for going to the United States, for good job prospects or family already established there.

The tribunal was, perhaps, reflecting a certain class bias when it suggested that any disbanded Irish

Above: Former RIC officer William Sidley became deputy inspector general of the Jamaica Constabulary Force, one of many Irish policemen who continued their service across the empire after 1921. (Sidley family)

policeman who was willing to work hard and move away from the cities would do well in the dominions, but it was correct to suggest that there was no guarantee of success. In September 1922, one ex-constable wrote to the *Weekly Irish Independent* that he and some colleagues, unable to find any work in Perth, Western Australia, were 'thinking of going back to Ireland, as we might as well be shot there as die here'. As is the case with all Irish migrants, broad and generalised depictions do not do justice to the range of experiences, successes and failures of this cohort of the Irish diaspora.

For those who left for Great Britain there was, potentially at least, solace and camaraderie to be found in numbers. Ex-RIC interest groups held social events, reunion dinners and dances throughout the 1920s. The Irish Office set up a body to assist arriving ex-policemen to find suitable accommodation, with headquarters in Cardiff and a branch in London. Chiefs of police were similarly instructed to do all they could to offer advice to former Irish policemen looking to 'settle in a strange town in Great Britain'. A group of ex-constables and their families formed their own 'little

Another ex-constable, Patrick Larkin, described his very different experience to the Irish Grants Committee: 'It is also very terrible to be walking around looking for work, nobody knows me to assist me, the result is that I get so fed-up, it is enough to make a man commit suicide. I find I am not able to get on here, not wanted in my own country, what am I to do?' In November 1922 the *Irish Times* reported the death by suicide of an 'unemployed and depressed' ex-constable in London.

The experiences of southern Irish loyalists of all shades, and their advocates, who moved literally and rhetorically across borders (including the Irish border), deserve their own place in any global history of the Irish Revolution.

Brian Hughes lectures in history at Mary Immaculate College, Limerick.

Further reading

F.M. Larkin, *Terror and discord: the Shemus cartoons in the* Freeman's Journal, *1920–1924* (Dublin, 2009).

R.B. McDowell, *Crisis and decline: the fate of the southern unionists* (Dublin, 1997).

M. Moulton, *Ireland and the Irish in interwar England* (Cambridge, 2014).

A TALE OF TWO CITIES:

EXPORTING THE IRISH REVOLUTION TO CHICAGO AND BUENOS AIRES

BY **DAVID BRUNDAGE**

In autumn 1920 Laurence Ginnell, the Dáil's director of propaganda, arrived in Chicago. His objective, like that of other republican emissaries, was to win the support of the Irish diaspora for the revolution at home. Ginnell's mission was generally successful. It was with high hopes that he set off the following July for Buenos Aires to take up his next assignment, but though he laboured diligently in the Argentine capital for nine months he faced disappointment at every turn. These dissimilar outcomes provide a window on the starkly different environments that republican envoys encountered among Irish emigrants and their descendants at various places around the globe.

Born to an agricultural labouring family in Delvin, Co. Westmeath, in 1852, Ginnell first came to prominence in the mid-to-late-1880s wave of agrarian agitation, the Plan of Campaign. Although a member of the English bar from 1893, he never practised law, dividing his time between politics and writing. He helped found the United Irish League in 1898 and ran unsuccessfully for parliament in 1900.

Ginnell was about the same age as the Irish Parliamentary Party's titans but, unlike them, he did not grow more conservative over time. While most IPP leaders celebrated the 1903 Land Purchase Act, Ginnell condemned it as the 'Landlord Relief Act' and in October 1906 introduced a new form of agrarian protest, in which crowds of small farmers and labourers drove the cattle of the big graziers off their land. Cattle-driving became a key tactic of the Ranch War (1904–8), the most important upsurge of agrarian conflict in the twentieth century, and Ginnell's role as a leading ranch warrior brought him wide renown. He was elected as MP for North Westmeath in 1906 and went on to serve twelve years in the House of Commons, where his dedication—along with a combativeness that one opponent considered 'one step removed from lunacy'—earned him the nickname 'member for Ireland'.

Ginnell continued to advocate cattle-driving, which led to his imprisonment in 1907–8. In 1909 the IPP expelled him, but he built an independent party organisation in north Westmeath that enabled him to win re-election as the self-proclaimed representative of 'the

Left: Westmeath Sinn Féin TD Larry Ginnell—the veteran radical laboured diligently for the Irish cause in Argentina but faced disappointment at every turn, illustrating the starkly different environments with which republican envoys dealt among the diaspora. (Library of Congress)

working classes'. Ginnell's radicalism extended to other issues: he was a prominent supporter of woman's suffrage and the first to oppose Redmond's recruiting efforts in autumn 1914.

Ginnell condemned the 1916 executions, worked tirelessly in Count Plunkett's February 1917 victory over the IPP in North Roscommon and by late 1917 was active in Sinn Féin leadership circles. He also continued to work on behalf of Ireland's rural poor, calling for the 'immediate restoration of all evicted tenants', the 'distribution of all ranches' and the 'amelioration of the conditions of agricultural labourers'. In March 1918 he was arrested again for cattle-driving.

Ginnell won election in the Sinn Féin landslide of December 1918 and, after his release from prison in March 1919, became the Dáil's first director of propaganda. He was arrested again in May, however, as part of the British crackdown on the revolutionary leadership and was jailed for another four months, after which he went on paid sick leave. In early autumn 1920 he departed for the United States, accompanied by his wife Alice (also a republican activist), to join the Irish mission that had been operating there since the previous year. More than a dedicated republican, Ginnell was an agrarian radical, with deep sympathies for Ireland's urban and rural poor. He would fit effortlessly into working-class Chicago, a place that poet Carl Sandburg had celebrated as the 'City of the Big Shoulders'.

Industrial Chicago was dominated by some of the largest corporations in the world, from meatpacking giants like Swift and Armour to US Steel, the first billion-dollar business in American history. It also had a tradition of labour militancy going back to the fight for the eight-hour day, the Haymarket bombing and the birth of May Day, the international workers' holiday, in the 1880s. A wartime organising drive in the stockyards and a bitterly fought (though unsuccessful) nationwide steel strike in 1919 had put Chicago at the centre of the post-First World War 'labour question'. It was also a city of tremendous ethnic and racial diversity—with Poles, Greeks, Slavs and African-American migrants from the Deep South finding work in the stockyards and the steel mills—but

●
Above left: John Fitzpatrick (standing)—the Athlone-born president of the Chicago Federation of Labor was deeply committed to Irish republicanism. He was also an opponent of racism, a supporter of female suffrage and a campaigner for Indian independence. (Library of Congress)

●
Left: Chicago stockyards, c. 1905—a centre for the US meatpacking industry, Chicago was a city of tremendous ethnic diversity, working class militancy and, in 1919, violent racial conflict. (Library of Congress)

also of sometimes-violent racial conflict. In July 1919 Chicago had been wracked by a major anti-black race riot that took the lives of 38 people.

Irish immigrants and their children, who accounted for nearly one out of every five of Chicago's residents by 1900, remained overwhelmingly working-class, but since they had arrived earlier than other groups they had already achieved prominence in politics, the police, the Catholic Church and, not least, the city's labour movement. At the centre of this movement was Athlone-born John Fitzpatrick, who became president of the Chicago Federation of Labor in 1905 and led it until his death in 1946. Famous for driving gangsters out of the labour movement, he was a key figure in the effort to bring trade unionism to new immigrant and African-American workers in steel and meatpacking during and after the First World War. He also advocated independent politics and, during Ginnell's stay in the city, was working to get the Farmer-Labor Party on its feet. Fitzpatrick supported Polish independence, female suffrage and freedom for India. He was a critic of the post-war 'red scare' and, like other left-wing progressives, called for US recognition of the new Russian Soviet government.

Fitzpatrick was also a deeply committed Irish republican. In autumn 1920 he was asked by the American Commission on Irish Independence to serve as president of its newly established Labor Bureau, and it was mainly to assist him in its work that Ginnell came to Chicago. Ginnell developed a list of American labour leaders sympathetic to the Irish republican cause and helped draft an 'appeal to American labor' that demanded immediate US recognition of the Irish Republic, condemned British atrocities and sought to enforce these positions by a labour-directed national boycott—a 'refusal to buy or handle English products or things carried in English ships'.

The response was overwhelming, with local labour councils in places from Portland, Maine, to Barstow, California, sending enthusi-

astic replies. Outside Chicago, Ginnell's main foray was to Washington DC, where in December 1920 he testified before the American Commission on Conditions in Ireland. A creation of the anti-imperialist American left, the Commission included liberal *Nation* editor Oswald Villard, socialist Norman Thomas and left-wing progressive Frederick Howe. With this sympathetic group as his audience, Ginnell's testimony focused on the importance of land redistribution in the Sinn Féin programme, catching the attention of the conservative *New York Times*, which ran the headline 'Irish Plan Republic on Socialist Basis'.

Ginnell's efforts culminated at the June 1921 convention of the American Federation of Labor, where Fitzpatrick launched an all-out effort to win support for a boycott of British goods. They were unsuccessful, although, as Harry Boland reported, the labour federation did pass 'very strong resolutions' in favour of an Irish republic. The following month, Ginnell wrapped up his American work and set off for Buenos Aires. The results had been gratifying and he had thrived in Chicago's progressive working-class milieu. He later (in March 1923) wrote to Fitzpatrick, expressing his deepest appreciation for 'the friendship I experienced from you and your colleagues'.

Ginnell's work in Argentina, however, where he held the title 'Envoy of the Republic of Ireland', was a study in frustration. It started off well enough. The Minister for Foreign Affairs granted him an audience and the Ginnells were honored at a 'High Mass for Ireland' and a reception at the Plaza Hotel (touted as the most elegant in South America) attended by a virtual 'who's who' of the Irish-Argentine community, including two national deputies and a descendant of the early nineteenth-century independence hero Admiral Guillermo Brown. In the following weeks, a stream of Irish-Argentine notables flooded into the mission office, which the Argentine-born 1916 veteran Eamonn Bulfin had opened in the stylish Galeria

Güemes the previous year. After announcing the Argentine bond drive for Ireland, Ginnell reported to Michael Collins that 'even people whom no one expected to be' were enthusiastic and that he hoped to raise as much as half a million pounds for the loan.

There were also numerous problems. First, Ginnell didn't speak Spanish. Second, though he tried to cultivate 'the best and wealthiest Irish-Argentines', he had not realised that, as the southern hemisphere's summer approached, many were leaving the capital for distant health resorts, where they would reside until March. A slump in the cattle market, a trade in which many wealthy Irish-Argentines were active, made everything more difficult. Ginnell was creative in his responses. He had his speeches translated into Spanish, memorising them word for word, and he worked closely with the editor of the Irish-Argentine weekly the *Southern Cross* to publicise developments in Ireland and coordinate a speaking tour outside the city.

By December 1921, however, prospects were dismal. According to Patrick Little, who joined Ginnell in September, 'the very rich Irish would be friendly today and tomorrow would be indifferent'. It was a constant struggle 'to get these people to keep up interest'. And, in a sharp contrast with Chicago, where Irish republicanism generated support among workers of diverse nationalities (including Poles and African-Americans), in Buenos Aires 'the Irish question is not alive among [the] working classes'.

Partly this was a problem of timing. Ginnell's Chicago work coincided with some of the most dramatic events of the Irish independence struggle, but he arrived in Argentina immediately after the July 1921 truce, which took the Irish question off the front burner. The sharply divergent history of the Irish diaspora in Argentina and the US was pertinent as well. First, the total number of people who emigrated to Argentina from Ireland was very small: from 1822 to 1929, less than 8,000 Irish immigrants arrived in

Buenos Aires. Second, the accumulation of wealth by a substantial number of this group marked a sharp contrast to Chicago, where the Irish were rooted mainly in the skilled working class and held dominant positions in the labour movement.

Argentina also had a strong labour movement and a tradition of popular political radicalism that actually surpassed the United States. It had elected the first socialist senator in the western hemisphere in 1913 and saw the founding of the second communist party in the world in 1918. Its anarchist movement was among the strongest anywhere, and syndicalists had taken control of its main labour federation, the Argentine Region Workers Federation, in 1915. Class conflict was often violent, as in the so-called *Semana Trágica* of January 1919, which began as a

Below: Argentinian Dáil bond (signed by Argentina-born Eamonn Bulfin)—Ginnell had hoped to raise half a million pounds among Argentina's well-established and often prosperous Irish community. (NAI)

general strike and ended up as a bloody anti-immigrant pogrom. And Buenos Aires, with its large port, meatpacking industry and multitude of small workshops, had just as big an immigrant working class as Chicago: 60% of its workers were foreign-born in 1914.

But it was Italian and Spanish—not Irish—immigrants who dominated labour and radical movements, and, to judge by editorials in the *Southern Cross*, Irish-Argentines were unrelentingly hostile to such movements. The paper's Offaly-born editor, Gerald Foley, regularly denounced strikes, socialists and Bolsheviks. In June 1921, just weeks before Ginnell's arrival, he gave full-throated support to a shadowy organisation made up of conservative employers and army officers called the Argentine Patriotic League, as it launched an attack targeting political radicals, immigrants and trades unionists. Little wonder, then, that the Irish question was not 'alive' among Argentina's working classes.

In sum, when Irish envoys like

Laurence Ginnell set out to advance the republican cause abroad, they found dramatically different situations in different places. The Irish independence struggle of 1918–23 unfolded in a revolutionary world that witnessed unprecedented levels of class conflict and new expressions of popular radicalism. The stance of Irish immigrants and their descendants in relation to these new trends could vary dramatically, however—which, in turn, affected the envoys' chances for success.

David Brundage is Professor of History at the University of California, Santa Cruz.

Further reading

D. Brundage, *Irish nationalists in America: the politics of exile, 1798–1998* (Oxford, 2016).

H. Kelly, *Irish 'Ingleses': the Irish immigrant experience in Argentina, 1840–1920* (Dublin, 2009).

M. Wheatley, *Nationalism and the Irish Party: provincial Ireland, 1910–1916* (Oxford, 2005).

DIASPORIC NATIONALISM ACROSS GENERATIONS:

IRISH REPUBLICANISM IN NEWFOUNDLAND

BY **PATRICK MANNION**

The small dominion of Newfoundland, one of the oldest outposts of the Irish Catholic diaspora, is an unlikely place to begin a history of the War of Independence. From the early eighteenth century, fishing vessels from the English West Country recruited labourers from the Irish south-east to work as servants in the Newfoundland cod fishery. This migration was initially seasonal, but after the collapse of the migratory fishery during the French Revolutionary Wars it evolved into permanent emigration. Some 35,000 Irish passengers arrived in the first third of the nineteenth century, an overwhelming majority from within 30 miles of the port of Waterford. Almost all were Catholic. Migration had virtually ceased by the early 1840s, and the vast numbers fleeing the Great Hunger bypassed Newfoundland.

By the beginning of the Anglo-Irish War, the Irish population of St John's, Newfoundland's capital and chief port (Newfoundland did not become a Canadian province until 1949), was several generations

●

Above: An Orange Lodge in Hamilton, Ontario, *c*. 1912—the Order in Canada regarded the Self-Determination for Ireland League as 'distinctly disloyal' and mobilised against it.

removed from the ancestral homeland. In 1921 there were just 127 Irish-born persons in the city out of a total population of 36,670 (0.3%), but the Catholic population of the town, almost exclusively of Irish descent, consisted of some 18,000 persons. We are dealing, then, with a substantial intergenerational ethnic community, in most cases several generations removed from Ireland and fully integrated into Newfoundland's social, economic and political structures. Nevertheless, Irish identities were raised to a fever pitch in 1920, when the establishment of the Self-Determination for Ireland League of Newfoundland (SDILN) prompted organised campaigns both for and against Irish independence. This passionate engagement with Irish nationalism in St John's calls into question the notion of an 'ethnic fade' within the North American diaspora. Irish identities did not necessarily wane generation by generation as assimilation occurred but rather rose and fell through time depending on circumstances in both the old world and the new. Moreover, even on the extreme north-east of the continent, the nationalist networks that mediated public engagement with Ireland were thoroughly North American, diffusing into the port city from the west.

The first extension of North American nationalist networks into St John's was the establishment of the republican Friends of Irish Freedom (FOIF) in late 1919 or early 1920. We know little of the 'Pádraig Pearse' branch—neither minutes of their meetings nor lists of members have survived. Newspaper reports suggest that the FOIF in St John's admitted between fifteen and twenty new members at each monthly meeting, but it is unlikely that the group exceeded 200 people at its peak. Its presence in St John's is nevertheless striking, as it represents a break with the predominantly constitutional interpretation of Irish nationalism that abounded in Newfoundland (and elsewhere in British North America) before the First World War. Unlike in Irish America, where republicanism was dominant, most individuals of Irish descent wished to extend to Ireland the same benefits and privileges that they enjoyed in the overseas dominions: self-government within the structures of the British Empire. Prior to the establishment of the FOIF, there is little evidence of support for a fully independent Irish republic in St John's.

Responding to this unexpected shift, Governor Charles Alexander Harris wrote to the colonial secretary, Viscount Milner, urging restraint: 'while it is doubtless very objectionable that a branch of an American Society … should be established in a British Colony, my view is that it is not well to take too much notice of the matter at present. I am clear that interference would only give undue prominence to the actions of such people.' The influence of the FOIF was ultimately limited in St John's, as most Catholic Newfoundlanders could not bring themselves to support its radical political objectives. Its presence, though, does show that the colony remained connected to the diasporic networks of Irish nationalism.

By far the most significant event in fostering widespread public engagement with the politics of Ireland in St John's was the visit of Irish-Canadian nationalist Katherine Hughes in October 1920. Born on Prince Edward Island of Irish Catholic descent, by 1920 Hughes was a committed republican working with the Friends of Irish Freedom in Washington. Owing to her Canadian origins, as well as her exceptional organisational and oratorical skills, Éamon de Valera selected her to establish an independent, pro-Sinn Féin organisation in Canada. The Self-Determination for Ireland League was formed in Montreal in May 1920 by Hughes and former Orangeman-turned-

Left: *The Quebec Chronicle* reports (30 August 1920) on the first provincial convention of the Self-Determination for Ireland League. Aware of both the strength of Canadian loyalism and the pro-imperial sentiments of many Irish Catholics, the League avoided committing openly to republicanism.

nationalist Lindsay Crawford. Keen to gain wide support and to avoid alienating Montreal's pro-imperial Irish Catholics, the new organisation adopted the non-committal objective of 'self-determination' for Ireland, rather than explicitly calling for Home Rule or an independent republic. With the structure of the League in place, Katherine Hughes embarked on a British North American tour to build support for the organisation.

In early October she arrived in St John's, where her visit generated tremendous interest. The groundwork had already been laid by Hughes's contacts in St John's, most notably a young lawyer, James O'Neill Conroy, whom Hughes later described as devoted to an Irish republic 'even to the point of *sacrifice*'. The first public lecture took place on 5 October at the Methodist College Hall. Over 1,000 people attended. Although privately Hughes advocated Ireland's full independence, her arguments in St John's were inherently couched in imperial terms. Hughes's key point was that self-determination for small nations like Ireland had been a central part of the Empire's war effort, and she made every effort to portray the new nationalist movement as situated fully within the boundaries of loyalty and respectability.

The following evening the Self-Determination for Ireland League of Newfoundland (SDILN) was formally established. R.T. McGrath, Newfoundland's chief customs inspector, was installed as chairman, and both local and dominion councils were named. Many of the dominion's most prominent Irish Catholics were involved, lending the new organisation considerable credibility. None of the League's leaders were born in Ireland. It was an entirely native-born executive. Hughes left Newfoundland with a positive impression:

'Both the organizational meeting and the public meeting were splendid. The latter was the most representative I have had outside of Washington ... Political leaders—the big men of the government—

the leader of the opposition, judges, editors, merchants, financiers, clergy, and of course the rank and file [were present]. Many converts to the cause were made.'

Newfoundlanders, she said, 'have the warmest Irish hearts I have met outside of Ireland ... Poor Newfoundland, so much like Ireland in kind hearts, in predominance of Irish blood and accent, and has also been a land of exploitation of the many by the few.'

The SDILN quickly emerged as the primary mechanism through which those of Irish descent in Newfoundland engaged with the movement for Irish independence. The substantial attention gained by Hughes's well-publicised tour as well as its broader, less radical objectives combined to make the SDILN a far more influential organisation than its FOIF predecessor. Through the League's networks, nationalists in Newfoundland worked closely with their counterparts in mainland Canada, facilitating the diffusion of stridently nationalist material into the port. J.M. Devine, a prominent tailor, and J.T. Meaney, Newfoundland's liquor inspector, represented the dominion at the League's national convention in Ottawa, where both gave rousing speeches. The dissemination of propaganda—supplied by the parent organisation in Ottawa—remained the League's primary function, as secretary Thomas Kelly submitted a series of articles in the final months of 1920 detailing Black-and-Tan atrocities in Ireland to the local newspapers. The League also held public meetings where various aspects of the Irish Question were discussed and debated. Women as well as men participated in these meetings—giving lectures, singing songs and reciting nationalist poetry. The most significant of these meetings was the visit of Canadian national president Lindsay Crawford in November 1920. Speaking to another capacity crowd at the Majestic Theatre, Crawford appealed for a 'broader spirit of toleration' regarding affairs in Ireland. The Irish Question, he said, was

neither 'racial nor religious in origin', and one did not have to be of Irish descent to support self-determination. Again, the League was actively attempting to build support for Irish independence from beyond the Irish Catholic community.

Despite the best efforts of Crawford and the SDILN to portray the self-determination movement as

Top: Katherine Hughes—Canadian-born, she was an exceptional public speaker and organiser, and a key figure in the Self-Determination for Ireland League.

Above: Archbishop Edward Roche of St John's—a Catholic imperialist, he feared that local activity on the Irish question could provoke a 'sectarian war'.

loyal and non-sectarian, by late 1920 support for, and opposition to, Irish independence was increasingly coalescing along denominational lines. The membership of the League appears to have been totally Catholic. James O'Neill Conroy informed Hughes that some members had gotten 'cold feet, owing to the fact that there are no Protestants in the League', adding that 'we have decided to go ahead without them'. The first moves against the SDILN were by Revd Dr Jones, a Presbyterian minister serving in St John's. He described the League as 'admittedly anti-British', and stated that all those 'who were imperial in their mindset would strongly and openly oppose it'.

As was the case in several Canadian cities around the same time, such as Halifax, Fredericton and Toronto, the movement against the SDILN gained institutional support through the networks of the Orange Order. At a special meeting on 1 December, the Provincial Grand Orange Lodge met to discuss the local situation. Orangemen from both St John's and the outports attended, with the meeting reportedly one of the largest in the organisation's history. The Order passed a formal resolution objecting to what they perceived as disloyalty on the part of civil servants and elected representatives:

'Whereas meetings of the [SDILN] have been held in the city of St John's, at which anti-British propaganda has been disseminated ... and whereas certain persons who occupy positions of employment under the Crown are prominently identified with the [SDILN] and have been guilty both at home and abroad of utterances which we regard as disloyal to the British Empire, be it therefore resolved that the Provincial Grand Orange

Above: Orangemen in Ontario, *c.* 1910—members of the Order dominated municipal politics in Toronto, which was known as the 'Belfast of Canada'.

Left: Newfoundland—a British colony until becoming a province of Canada in 1949. By the beginning of the Anglo-Irish War, its Irish population was several generations removed from the ancestral homeland.

Lodge of Newfoundland now in session and representing over twenty thousand loyal citizens, believes that the object of the Self-Determination for Ireland League of Newfoundland, and similar organizations, is to have Ireland secede from the British Empire and become a Republic, and regards the Self-Determination League as a distinctly disloyal movement … wholly unworthy of men and women who are enjoying the liberties and privileges of the British Constitution.'

The resolution concluded by demanding that any civil servants associated with the League be dismissed.

Over the following weeks, into the winter and spring of 1921, numerous letters both supporting and opposing the SDILN appeared in local papers. Newfoundland's ultra-imperialist Catholic archbishop, Edward Roche, wrote to McGrath urging caution in any public response to the Orangemen so as to avoid in Newfoundland 'the throes of a sectarian war'. The concern in Roche's letter is evident, while Governor Harris wrote to the new colonial secretary, Winston Churchill, suggesting that the British government produce a pamphlet to be circulated in Newfoundland and other domin-ions to counter Irish nationalist propaganda and redeem Britain's reputation amongst disillusioned Catholics of Irish descent.

The tensions in St John's eased considerably following the truce in July 1921. The SDILN remained publicly silent and did not comment on the negotiations that led to the Anglo-Irish Treaty in December of that year. The League's structure endured, however, and it continued to connect those of Irish descent to the broader diaspora. In 1922, McGrath selected a young St John's-born law student at Oxford, William J. Browne, to represent Newfoundland at the Irish Race Congress in Paris. Several months later, the SDILN helped fund marathon-runner Jack Bell to attend Aonach Tailteann—the Irish Race Olympics—in Dublin. Bell arrived in Ireland in August, only to find the meet cancelled owing to the Irish Civil War. After this point public activities by the SDILN ceased, and a final meeting was held to wind up its affairs in May 1923.

We cannot be sure how many paid-up members actually joined the SDILN, but thousands of individuals of Irish descent took part in its meetings, lectures and rallies in 1920 and 1921, while hundreds more travelled from across the island to oppose it. It was far from being a small, isolated movement. The dramatic rise and fall of the SDILN in St John's reveals both the spatial and generational spread of early twentieth-century diasporic nationalism. A sense of 'being Irish' clearly persisted for many Newfoundland Irish Catholics, but in the opening two decades of the twentieth century this had rarely served as a basis for a cohesive group identity. The visit of Katherine Hughes in October 1920 was the seminal event in prompting an Irish resurgence. As nationalist literature and speakers arrived in St John's from mainland Canada, the League's structures transformed private ethnic indignation into an active participation in diasporic nationalism. This renewed sense of Irish identity, though, was fleeting, as the furore surrounding the League died down almost as quickly as it had emerged. Irish ethnicity, therefore, did not decline in a linear fashion but rather rose and fell through time and across generations. Despite being, in many cases, four or more generations removed from their ancestral homeland, the SDILN ensured that the intergenerational Irish of Newfoundland remained part of the diasporic movement for Irish freedom.

Patrick Mannion was a Social Sciences and Humanities Research Council of Canada postdoctoral fellow in the Department of History at Boston College, 2016–18, and is currently a per-course instructor in the Department of History at Memorial University of Newfoundland.

Further reading

R. McLaughlin, *Irish Canadian conflict and the struggle for Irish independence, 1912–1925* (Toronto, 2013).

P. Mannion, *A land of dreams: ethnicity, nationalism, and the Irish in Newfoundland, Nova Scotia, and Maine, 1880–1923* (Montreal and Kingston, 2018).

P. Ó Siadhail, *Katherine Hughes: a life and a journey* (Newcastle, 2014).

●

Above: Sir Charles Alexander Harris (1855–1947), governor of Newfoundland from 1917–22. In response to the establishment of a branch of the Friends of Irish Freedom in the colony he said, 'I am clear that interference would only give undue prominence to the actions of such people'.

'AT THE OUTPOSTS OF EMPIRE':
AUSTRALASIAN PERSPECTIVES ON THE IRISH REVOLUTION

BY **RORY SWEETMAN**

Left: Painting of Archbishop Daniel Mannix of Melbourne by Clifton Pugh. A former president of St Patrick's College, Maynooth, the Cork-born Mannix played a major role in opposing conscription in Australia and supporting Irish independence.

Opposite page: *The Vigilant*, published by the Victoria Protestant Federation in Australia. Loyalist opposition to Irish republicanism, often expressed in sectarian terms, was a force throughout the Empire. (Jimmy Yan)

The impact of the global Irish diaspora on the Irish Revolution is easier to assess in relation to North America than to Australia and New Zealand. Weight of numbers and proximity prompted a deep involvement by Irish Americans in Irish affairs. Irish nationalists—constitutional and revolutionary—depended on Irish America both for inspiration and for hard cash. During 1919–21 there was fierce competition for American sympathies as the Irish Republic strove to assert its claim to international recognition. A host of delegates from Ireland toured North America (most notably Éamon de Valera in 1919–20) in order to enlist support for Irish separatism. While the goal of an unambiguous endorsement of the Irish Republic proved elusive, huge sums were collected to fuel the campaign in Ireland, and it has been argued that American support encouraged a bolder, more aggressive Irish struggle for independence from Britain.

By contrast, historians have tended to downplay the role of the antipodean Irish in these stirring events. They were fewer and much further away—an isolated, unpopular minority camped in British dominions, in Patrick O'Farrell's words, 'reliant on the empire for defence, status, self-image and cultural orientation'. Overwhelmingly identified as Catholics despite a sizeable Protestant component, they were also stereotyped as poor, ignorant, drunken and criminal—figures of fun and fear by turn. Unlike their American cousins, they were not fleeing from famine nor did they cluster in ghettoes, a disadvantaged proletariat with a burning hatred for perfidious Albion. The Irish in the antipodes were a founding people who eagerly embraced their new economic opportunities and showed scant interest in Irish separatism. They would respond to genuine Irish distress and turn up in droves to hear itinerant Irish nationalist delegates, but displayed little of the Anglophobia that characterised much of Irish America.

While Fenianism found few colonial supporters, Home Rule in the later nineteenth and early twentieth centuries had a huge appeal. It allowed Irish emigrants to reconcile their dual loyalties: Ireland would be both free and a loyal member of the imperial family. Irish nationalist spokesmen who visited the antipodes in these years recognised the difference between the expatriate worlds by moderating their speech while in the southern hemisphere, cutting the cloth of Irish national ambitions to a colonial measure. Both of New Zealand's political leaders during the First World War trod warily on the Irish issue: the Ulster-born William Massey, a prominent Orangeman, kept largely silent on Irish Home Rule, while his rival, Sir Joseph Ward, an Irish Catholic, flaunted his imperialism. By 1914 it appeared that the old Irish roles were reversed, as the Ulster unionist campaign posed a German-supported threat to the Empire, while colonial Irish nationalists prepared to celebrate the reopening of the Irish parliament on College Green.

The First World War and the Easter Rising of 1916 appeared to restore the Irish contenders to their accustomed roles: while Ulster Protestants perished for the Empire at the Somme, Irish Catholic rebels had stabbed it in the back with German aid. The Irish in Australasia initially deplored events in Dublin but soon began to condemn the British post-Rising repression, thus mirroring public opinion in Ireland. A period of unusually intense involvement by the diaspora in Irish affairs began in 1916, a sustained participation led by Irish-born clergy in the international war of words that eventually drove Britain to the negotiating table. By downplaying its significance, Australian historians

The Vigilant

The Official Organ of the Victorian Protestant Federation

Registered at the G.P.O., Melbourne, for transmission as a newspaper

Vol. II.   No. 11   .   THURSDAY, MARCH 17, 1921.   Price, One Penny

GREAT LOYALIST DEMONSTRATION

Melbourne Town Hall   -   Sinn Fein Resolution Condemned

have underestimated the depth, meaning and effectiveness of this antipodean contribution.

Colonial harmony was regularly disrupted by waves of radical Irish immigrants, who forced the diaspora community back into the trenches. Two clerical firebrands arrived in 1913: Daniel Mannix and James Kelly. Mannix (coadjutor archbishop of Melbourne) became a celebrated figure, equally revered and reviled in both Ireland and Australia, while Kelly (editor of the *New Zealand Tablet*, 1917–31) languishes in comparative obscurity. They both left a resurgent Catholic Ireland for what they regarded as a benighted British Protestant colony in which their co-religionists were apparently enduring second-class citizenship. By interpreting local Catholic grievances in Irish terms, they helped to drag diaspora opinion away from constitutionalism and towards the new Irish nationalist orthodoxy, Sinn Féin.

Most of the dozen or so biographies of Mannix chart his balanced response to the Easter Rising and his early backing of Sinn Féin. He hosted an Irish Race Convention in November 1919, and later met and personally endorsed de Valera in the US before being 'arrested' *en route* to Ireland and banned from visiting his native land. According to O'Farrell,

Mannix's followers supported him as a *Catholic* rather than as an Irish leader. While they applauded his confrontational style and echoed his cry of 'Australia First', Ireland was for them merely a symbol, masking local antagonisms. Without him, 'it seems likely that the issues of Irish rebellion and independence would have received small attention in Australia. Most Irish-Australians would have preferred to avoid them, but Mannix made this impossible.'

Can the same be said of James Kelly in New Zealand? A reluctant emigrant, Kelly held strong views on Ireland's destiny, which were expressed in his *Tablet* columns through torrents of Anglophobia. His anti-British diatribes were so savage that (after only nine issues from his pen) New Zealand's solicitor-general advised the government to suppress the *Tablet* and prosecute its editor for sedition. Kelly had initially dismissed the Easter Rising as 'mad, bad and sad', although he added that 'Maxwellian monstrosities made heroes of those who were only fools'. Less than a year later, however, he was lauding the 1916 leaders, who 'died like men, bearing the punishment for the faults of all'. Bitterly disillusioned by John Redmond's apparent willingness to bargain away Ireland's territorial integrity, Kelly

as various American and Australian Catholic papers and British sources like the *New Witness*, the *Nation*, the *Glasgow Observer* and *Stead's Review*. Their denunciations of Black-and-Tan atrocities enabled Kelly to gloss over the very real problem of IRA violence. He was importunate in his demands. 'Do not weep for Erin,' he urged his readers; rather ask 'what are we going to do to save her?' Kelly was furious that New Zealand, alone of the self-governing dominions, had failed to raise its voice for Irish freedom. In mid-1921 he expressed the fear that 'the last Black and Tan will have been driven out of Ireland while we are dreaming and we shall have had no share in the deliverance'.

Under Kelly's able generalship, the Irish-descended Catholic community stood up to be counted, gathering in their thousands at St Patrick's Day functions, writing letters to the press, passing inspired resolutions, wearing Sinn Féin badges and waving the tricolour. Although never able to force through a parliamentary resolution in favour of Irish self-determination, Kelly raised colonial awareness of Irish realities and funnelled considerable financial resources back to Ireland. His activities give an insight into the mechanics of revolutionary networks and diasporic nationalism in what was a fierce competition for the hearts and minds of Britain's white dominions. As Sinn Féin and Dáil Éireann placed their case before the world, the Irish abroad were exposed to a stream of

was ecstatic over Sinn Féin's electoral victory in December 1918. 'The end of the year has brought our justification. The lying press that told its readers constantly that the Sinn Féin movement did not represent the Irish people has had its answer now.' He attended the Irish Race Convention in Melbourne, which pledged 'to support Ireland's claim as expressed at the last general election in Ireland and to support her chosen leader, Éamon de Valera'.

'Knowing Ireland and being in constant touch', Kelly was able to interpret the complexity of Irish political developments for his colonial audience. His correspondents included his cousins, the Ryans of Tomcoole (prominent within revolutionary circles), Bishop Fogarty (of Killaloe) and William O'Brien MP, leader of the moderate All-for-Ireland League. He regularly cited the *Catholic Bulletin*, *Nationality*, the *Leader*, *New Ireland* and the *Irish Bulletin*, as well

Above left: Pro-conscription campaigners in Mingenew, Western Australia, 1917—the Irish Catholic vote was judged to have contributed to its defeat in plebiscites in October 1916 and December 1917. (Wikipedia)

Left: Revd James Kelly—the Irish-born cleric and editor of the *New Zealand Tablet* denounced British policy in language so savage that the country's solicitor-general demanded that he be prosecuted for sedition.

Opposite page: William (Bill) Massey—the Limavady-born prime minister of New Zealand refused to allow de Valera, whom he described as 'a traitor and a disloyal man', to visit the country. (Alexander Turnbull Library, Wellington, NZ)

information, propaganda and personalities, Irish Race Conventions and fund-raising appeals. Both sides understood the need to shape the overseas perception of Irish events. Colonial opinion was of great importance to British politicians both during and after the war, with recurrent suggestions that the dominion premiers might play a role in finding an Irish solution. Delegates toured the US and Australasia presenting the Irish unionist case, along with an avalanche of anti-Sinn Féin propaganda.

While Prime Minister Massey refused to allow de Valera ('a traitor and a disloyal man') to enter New Zealand, his emissary Katherine Hughes was able to visit both countries to found the Self-Determination for Ireland League of Australasia. Kelly welcomed Hughes and even moderated his language, insisting that Ireland had not yet been offered dominion home rule. The League grew rapidly, as it also offered a home to those whose sympathy for the cause did not encompass an Irish republic. The search for allies outside the Catholic community helped to draw Kelly closer to the emergent New Zealand Labour Party (founded in 1916), which raised a series of parliamentary motions critical of British policy in Ireland and which were designed to needle Massey and his Reform Party government. The NZLP was encouraged by the British Labour Party's 'Peace with Ireland Campaign' in 1920–1, involving public meetings, questions in the House of Commons and a commission of inquiry into the Irish question. Kelly was delighted by the NZLP's stance. 'We are their debtors, as is every Irishman, and every man of Irish blood in New Zealand, and we do not forget it.'

Other less friendly groups also took up the Irish issue. The Protestant Political Association (an offshoot of the New Zealand Orange Order) detected a papal plot against Protestantism and Empire. Such conspiracy theories flourished in a climate of smothering conformity and paranoia during and after the war. Irish Catholics found themselves increasingly the victims of a narrowing definition of loyalty, with frequent paeans to empire masking a British patriotism intolerant of any rival. The refusal to countenance any critique of Britishness was demonstrated in March 1922, after a speech by Bishop James Liston in the Auckland Town Hall referring to 'that glorious Easter' of 1916 and lauding those Irishmen whom he claimed had been 'murdered by foreign troops'. Following an overwhelmingly hostile public outcry, Liston was charged with sedition and had to endure a two-day trial in the supreme court. The Catholic community mobilised in Liston's support, even threatening to offer physical resistance should he be convicted and jailed. Despite his native birth, the bishop's professions of pride in and love for New Zealand were deemed insufficient to excuse his remarks. Nevertheless, the judge and jury that acquitted him were in no doubt as to the culpability of the Black-and-Tans in Ireland, Justice Stringer declaring, 'It is notorious that when reprisals were in progress the Black and Tans committed murders. Everybody knows that.'

Press censorship in Ireland meant that the sharpest attacks on British policy were made by correspondents from British newspapers. Revd John Dickie, a Scots-born professor at Dunedin's Presbyterian Theological College and one of Kelly's fiercest critics, complained that such reports were 'showing the whole situation in a false perspective'. His long article in the *National Review* (1921) accused the British government of unpardonable weakness and of letting down its colonial supporters 'at the outposts of Empire'. Further shocks were in store for Dickie, as Liberal Prime Minister David Lloyd George and his colleagues began negotiating with men they had earlier denounced as a 'murder gang'. The subsequent Anglo-Irish Treaty was greeted with widespread relief on all sides in New Zealand and Australia, followed by general confusion and dismay at the slide towards civil war. Kelly wrote to William O'Brien: 'We think the agreement arrived at ought to be accepted. It is more than half a

loaf and we do not like the risk of turning it down and getting no bread instead.'

As the heroes of the Irish Revolution turned their guns upon each other, few were prepared to follow Mannix into the wilderness by supporting the anti-Treatyites. The fratricidal conflict effectively marked the end of the Irish question as a major issue in New Zealand and Australia. When two republican emissaries approached New Zealand in 1925, Bishop Brodie (of Christchurch) remarked tartly, 'I leave the affairs of Ireland to the Irish in Ireland'.

Rory Sweetman is a Kildare-born New Zealander with degrees in history from Dublin and Cambridge Universities. His latest book analyses the defence of Trinity College Dublin during the 1916 Rising.

Further reading

P. O'Farrell, *The Irish in Australia* (Sydney, 1986).

P. O'Farrell, *Vanished kingdoms. Irish in Australia and New Zealand* (Sydney, 1990).

R. Sweetman, *Bishop in the dock. The sedition trial of James Liston in New Zealand* (Dublin, 2006).

EMPIRE
AND ANTI-IMPERIALISM

Are they willing on their part to give the right of self-determination to the peoples of Ireland, Egypt, India, Madagascar, Indochina … ? For it is clear that to demand self-determination for the peoples that are comprised within the borders of enemy states and to refuse self-determination to the peoples of their own state or of their own colonies would mean the defence of the most naked, the most cynical imperialism.

—Leon Trotsky, Bolshevik Commissar for Foreign Affairs, 29 December 1918

Image: 'THE FLAGS OF A FREE EMPIRE, SHOWING THE EMBLEMS OF BRITISH POWER THROUGHOUT THE WORLD' by Arthur Mee, 1910. (Cornell University)

THE REVOLUTION AS TURNING POINT? IRISH ACTORS ON AN IMPERIAL STAGE

BY **TIMOTHY G. McMAHON**

The era of the Irish Revolution (1916–23) cemented the impression that Irish nationalism was an anti-imperial movement, but nationalism's connection to anti-imperialism was less straightforward than might be assumed. Part of the explanation for the conflation of nationalism with anti-imperialism can be found in the coincidence of Ireland's achieving a degree of independence amid the general call for the breakup of empires that took place during and after the Great War. But two additional factors also shaped this presumed link. First, during the nineteenth and early twentieth centuries, tension existed between those in Ireland who saw empire as a source of opportunity and those who considered it an inherent evil. The revolutionary period saw the emergence of a leadership cadre more clearly tied to anti-colonial sentiment at home and to championing the breakup of the British Empire throughout the world than had been the case throughout the previous century. Second, the leaders of unionism in Northern Ireland distinguished themselves from their nationalist counterparts in the Irish Free State by emphasising their staunch support for the British Empire. Nonetheless, as had been the case for their forerunners, twentieth-century Irish nationalists included empire-builders as well as anti-imperialists.

Although the British Empire was the most important imperial entity associated with Ireland, it was not the only one. Especially during the early modern period, dispossessed Irish élites found opportunities in the service of Continental powers (including Spain, Austria and France) in building and maintaining their empires. Within the British Empire, positions in the armed forces, in the colonial service, in trade or in the mission field appealed to Irish people of all denominations. In the nineteenth century many achieved distinction, including the Tipperary-born Lt. Gen. Sir William Francis Butler, who became the highest-ranking Catholic in the army, and the 6th earl of Mayo, Richard Southwell Bourke, who served as viceroy of India from 1869 to 1872. His assassination inspired massive funerals in Calcutta and Dublin, as well as collections that financed construction of a large home on his family's estate at Palmerstown, Co. Kildare, and memorials in Ireland, Britain and India.

Moreover, Catholic missionary orders recruited extensively in Ireland to spread their message under the umbrella of an empire led by the titular head of the Anglican Communion. Especially in the decades after the Great Hunger—when emigration to Britain, its colonies of settlement and the United States became so much a feature of the Irish experience—the Vatican called on English-speaking

Left: William Hoey Kearney Redmond MP (1861–1917) (with his brother John, leader of the Irish Parliamentary Party) in 1912— few public figures bridged seemingly contradictory pro- and anti-imperial positions more clearly. (NLI)

Irish clergy and religious to staff their burgeoning dioceses. Little wonder that Colin Barr has described these new structures, shaped significantly by Cardinal Paul Cullen's network of relatives and followers, as a 'Hiberno-Roman Church'.

Alongside such opportunities stood the ongoing critique of imperial power, through constitutional parties, revolutionary activity and popular sensibilities at home and in the Irish diaspora. Anti-imperial messages in newspapers often compared wars on the imperial frontier with earlier campaigns against the Irish. Indeed, as Paul Townend has shown, opposition to military actions in southern Africa, Egypt, the Sudan and Afghanistan was an essential link between popular agitation and the parliamentary campaign for Home Rule under Charles Stewart Parnell in the late 1870s and early 1880s.

Few public figures bridged these seemingly contradictory positions more clearly than William Hoey Kearney Redmond MP (1861–1917). From a family with a tradition of military service in the British Army, he joined the Wexford militia battalion of the Royal Irish Rifles as a young man. Like his brother John, leader of the Irish Parliamentary Party in the early 1900s, William Redmond travelled widely to raise

●
Above left: 'THIS HOUSE WAS BUILT IN HONOURED MEMORY OF RICHARD SIXTH EARL OF MAYO K.P G.M.S.I VICEROY AND GOVERNOR GENERAL OF INDIA BY HIS FRIENDS AND COUNTRYMEN A.D 1872'—inscription above the entrance to Palmerstown House, Johnstown, Co. Kildare. Now a wedding venue with an adjacent golf course, it was burnt down by anti-Treaty forces in 1923.

●
Left: Detail of a commemorative mural at Jallianwala, Amritsar, Punjab, depicting the massacre of April 1919. The mass shooting of civilians at Croke Park in November 1920 was referred to by Irish republicans variously as 'Bloody Sunday' or 'Ireland's Amritsar'.

●
Opposite page: Tipperary-born Sir Michael O'Dwyer, lieutenant-governor of the Punjab at the time of the Amritsar massacre, was disdainful of Indian nationalist protest. (NPG)

money from émigré communities for the Home Rule cause. He married an Australian-Irish woman and came to appreciate what he saw as the positive legacies of those who populated various corners of the world. He celebrated the Australian leg of one such trip in the book *Through the new Commonwealth* (1906), essentially making the case that a Home Rule Ireland would prosper and co-operate in the wider imperial enterprise.

Among the sites that impressed him deeply was a recently built memorial to the 'Wicklow Chief', Michael Dwyer (1772–1825), and the United Irish rebels of 1798 at Waverly Cemetery, which points to his more critical view of the Empire. Redmond frequently linked the land and anti-imperial causes throughout his career. Indeed, he served three stints in jail for his commitment to land agitation (1882, 1888 and 1902) and he made fiery anti-imperialist speeches, defending the Mahdi in the mid-1880s and denouncing aggression against the Boers in 1899. His pro-Boer rhetoric even led to his expulsion from the House of Commons that October. Such actions did not silence him, however, and he became treasurer of the Irish Transvaal Committee, connecting him with proponents of the nascent republican and labour movements such as Arthur Griffith, Maud Gonne and James Connolly.

These seemingly contradictory sensibilities reflected Redmond's background and experiences as a socially conscious person of privilege. He was especially concerned that those with more power not subjugate those with less. He also believed that recognition of the Irish demand for Home Rule would, as he told the House of Commons in December 1912, make the 'Irish soldier, like the Irish race, for the first time in their history, into the friends and not the disaffected subjects of the British Empire'. These words, however, came at a time when Home Rule was being challenged by a still-small body of radical nationalists, who wanted a complete break from monarchical

government and the imperial project, and by Irish unionists whose cooperation with British Conservatives was based, in part, on the conviction that any concession to nationalism would undermine the United Kingdom's imperial destiny.

The Great War and the revolutionary years witnessed a series of events that fundamentally altered Ireland's relationship to the Empire. Although Home Rule received the royal assent in the first weeks of the war, the Liberal government of H.H. Asquith suspended it for the conflict's duration. Then, at Easter 1916, a faction of the underground Irish Republican Brotherhood spearheaded a rebellion centred on Dublin. In its wake, the government arrested more than 3,400 people throughout Ireland, many of whom had had no connection with the violence. Further, Asquith deputised David Lloyd George to negotiate activating Home Rule, a pivotal moment for two reasons.

First, to ease unionist concerns, he promised party leaders that six of Ulster's nine counties would remain governed from Westminster rather than from Dublin, but he presented this partition option to nationalists and unionists in very different ways. Those differences undermined the negotiations, but not before six-county partition had been mooted seriously for the first time. When it recurred four years later in the Better Government of Ireland Act (1920), the six-county unit, known as Northern Ireland, was to have its own Home Rule parliament, just as the 26-county entity envisioned would have a parliament for domestic affairs. Especially in its earliest years, the leadership of the Northern state emphasised their loyalty to the Empire, in part to distinguish themselves from the nationalist leadership of the Dublin-based government.

Second, the failure of the 1916 negotiations reinforced the sense that Home Rulers could not deliver for their increasingly restive constituents. The Irish Parliamentary Party had entered the war years

believing that domestic self-government would come shortly via their Liberal allies but saw their goal repeatedly postponed. Moreover, battlefront casualties took away some of the party's leading pre-war voices, including that of William Redmond, who died in Belgium in June 1917. Angry and disenchanted nationalist voters, therefore, came to consider alternatives to the old party.

In a series of by-elections in 1917 and in the general election at the war's end, a new leadership cadre emerged. Led by Éamon de Valera (1882–1975), who won the by-election for Redmond's East Clare constituency, the Sinn Féin party spoke of creating an Irish republic and of gaining international recognition through an appeal to the concept of national self-determination. Its victorious candidates created the first Dáil Éireann in January 1919 and declared Ireland independent. Meanwhile, loosely affiliated but increasingly coordinated provincial companies of Irish Volunteers struck against the agents of the Crown. The guerrilla war that developed over the next two years featured outbursts of appalling violence, the use of prisons and prison camps to hold combatants, and simmering uncertainty for the non-combatant population.

Such events mirrored concurrent experiences throughout the Empire. Indeed, in 1919 and 1920 alone, violent and non-violent nationalist campaigns erupted in Egypt, India and Mesopotamia, and on the Afghanistan–India border. One of the most notorious incidents of these years occurred in the Punjab, where Sir Michael O'Dwyer, the lieutenant-governor and a graduate of the Redmonds' Alma Mater, Clongowes Wood College, treated protests and protesters with disdain. Then, in mid-April 1919, the Cork-educated Brig. Gen. Reginald Dyer ordered troops to fire into a crowd gathered for a Sikh festival in Amritsar, killing hundreds. This shocking moment became both the standard by which large-scale violence was judged and the ready shorthand by which those labelling violent outbursts condemned them. For instance, Irish republicans referred to the mass shooting of civilians at Croke Park in November 1920 variously as 'Bloody Sunday' or 'Ireland's Amritsar'.

Ultimately, because the Irish campaign led to the creation of the Irish Free State, imperial and anti-colonial advocates in the mid-twentieth century looked to the island as a type of testing ground. To be sure, imperial opportunism continued quietly under the new dispensation, as colonial police services and the British colonial office still recruited extensively in both Northern Ireland and the Free State. Equally important, though, the Free State and its successor states became touchstones for nationalists elsewhere, reinforcing the contrast implied by Northern Ireland unionists. Particularly after de Valera and his followers asserted that Ireland stood outside the Empire in the 1930s, activists in Asia and Africa found inspiration for their own struggles in Ireland's apparent successes. Some, including India's Jawaharlal Nehru, Burma's Chan Htoon and Ghana's Kwame Nkrumah, visited Dublin (as is explored elsewhere in this volume by Ken Shonk), and Irish diplomats consulted with those establishing new states and constitutions. And even mission work—which could be viewed from one angle as a cultural hold-over from the days of presumed European superiority—could also carry with it overtones of devotion and liberation. Such was the case with the former schoolteacher Nora Loughnane, whose brothers Patrick and Harry were captured, tortured and killed by Black-and-Tans in a vicious incident in 1920 in south Galway. She later joined the missionary convent at Ardfoyle, Co. Cork, took the name Sister Patricia in honour of her elder brother and served in the Gold Coast in the later 1920s.

Understanding these ongoing ambivalences, reshaped though they were in the revolutionary years, will be one of the most important new waves of research into Ireland's complex relationship with the imperial world.

Timothy G. McMahon is an Associate Professor in History at Marquette University.

Further reading

T.G. McMahon, M. de Nie & P. Townend (eds), *Ireland in an imperial world: citizenship, opportunism, and subversion* (London, 2017).

P. Townend, *The road to Home Rule: anti-imperialism and the Irish national movement* (Madison, 2016).

M. Walsh, *Bitter freedom: Ireland in a revolutionary world, 1918–1923* (London, 2015).

Below: The mutilated remains of brothers Patrick and Harry Loughnane (left), tortured and killed in a notorious incident by Black-and-Tans in south Galway in November 1920. Their sister Nora (right) became a missionary in the Gold Coast and took the name Sister Patricia in honour of her elder brother. (*African Missionary*, January 1929)

IRELAND AND EGYPT:

ANTI-IMPERIALISM AT BAY

BY **KATE O'MALLEY**

The year 1919 was a turning point in British imperial history. It witnessed anti-British revolutions in Ireland, India and Egypt, while the following year political conflict erupted in Iraq. This period also saw the spread of Bolshevism abroad, agitation and post-war malaise at home, and the beginning of sustained political unrest in India. All these factors came together to reinforce the general perception of a British Empire in irreversible decline. While much research has been carried out into links between Irish and Indian nationalism, little is known about whether Egyptian nationalists ever looked to Ireland as an example and, if so, whether they found any common ground.

News of the establishment of Dáil Éireann reached far beyond Europe and countries that had a large Irish diaspora. Sir Percy Cox, the British minister in Tehran, who was then negotiating the short-lived Anglo-Persian Agreement, was alarmed at the impact that news from Ireland was having. The Shah approached Cox after hearing reports of the establishment of a republican

Above: Egyptian women on the streets of Cairo during the 1919 revolution, events that were followed keenly by Irish republicans.

government in Dublin and its declaration of independence. Cox replied that 'as far as I could see it only amounted to vapouring on the part of the Irish extremists which His Majesty's Government did not regard seriously, and that there was no cause for superlative disquietude'. His statement created an unfavourable impression, however, and he was asked to request an authoritative explanation from His Majesty's government.

The Shah's scepticism proved well founded. The four years that followed 1919 witnessed a political and military struggle within Ireland against British rule: the Irish War of Independence. The Dáil government's Department of Foreign Affairs and a republican diplomatic service were established in these turbulent years. The primary object of this nascent department was to gain international recognition for the Irish Republic. The Dáil's first step in this direction was to send a team to the Paris peace conference of 1919 to lobby for recognition of the Irish Republic and separate Irish admission to the conference.

One of the first Sinn Féin envoys, and later Minister for Foreign Affairs, was George Gavan Duffy. Duffy, a lawyer who spoke numerous languages, had been educated in both France and England. He had already established firm contacts within the Egyptian and Indian communities in Europe through the activities of the International Subject Races Committee. Dublin-born activist Nanny Florence Dryhurst was the committee's honorary secretary. Its first conference was held in London in June 1910 and saw demands for Home Rule in Ireland and India. It was through the committee's meetings that Duffy met the Egyptian leader Mohammad Farid. The two men would meet again almost ten years later on the peripheries of the peace conference. Before that, Duffy had been solicitor for Roger Casement, who, in the immediate outbreak of the First World War, had gone to Germany to recruit an Irish brigade from Irish prisoners of war there. Casement told his recruits that 'a shot fired for Ireland's freedom in Egypt could be as good as a shot fired in Ireland', and encouraged them to volunteer for service with the German expeditionary forces in the Mediterranean.

Casement's later trial and his subsequent execution affected Duffy deeply. He left the salubrious surroundings of London for a tumultuous Dublin and became immersed in Irish politics. He won a seat in the 1918 general election and was sent to Paris to join Seán T. Ó Ceallaigh, another leading Sinn Féin leader, as an envoy seeking recognition for the Irish Republic from French Prime Minister Georges Clemenceau and admittance to the peace conference itself. In May 1919 the Paris delegation was given clear instructions from Éamon de Valera to develop contacts with sympathetically minded anti-imperialists.

● Above: 'Crowds in Cairo fly an American flag during the revolution of 1919—as in Ireland, President Wilson's promise of self-determination offered great hope of change.

● Opposite page: Nationalist leader Saad Zaghloul posing for a sculptor in 1926. In 1919 Lloyd George had been warned that the Egyptian would 'create a Pan-Islamic-Sinn Féin machine making mischief everywhere'. (Alamy)

Duffy's own observations on who best to seek out in Paris provide illuminating evidence of the benefits of his earlier experiences in London networking against the Empire.

'I don't think that [a league of small nations] is feasible because most of the small nations have their own hands to play and are mightily afraid of entangling alliances or associations at present. There would be much more chance of co-operation against the Union Jack of Boers, Egyptians and ourselves with the Indians, if they can get here, and any views of the Cabinet on this and the pros and cons would be useful.'

After the outbreak of the First World War, Britain unilaterally declared a protectorate over Egypt; then, in the wake of the war, there began in Egypt a popular move towards the establishment of a constitutional monarchy. When an Egyptian delegation (or 'Wafd') made attempts to travel to the post-war peace conference in Paris, however, its leaders were arrested and deported to Malta. This resulted in widespread outrage in Egypt.

The ensuing Egyptian revolution of 1919 received considerable attention in Ireland. Occurring in the spring of 1919, it coincided with the outbreak of the Irish War of Independence. Reports of trouble elsewhere in the British Empire were bound to gain attention in Ireland. Numerous articles in the press drew comparisons between the situations in Ireland and Egypt, with one of the leading dailies, the *Irish Independent*, calling the upheaval in Egypt 'a second Ireland'. The *Evening Herald* reported that the demonstrations and resultant rioting in Egypt were 'reminiscent of recent happenings in Ireland'. By April 1919 the British had given way to Egyptian protesters, allowing a delegation to go to Paris. By that time the peace conference was in full swing, and the Irish press were reporting that the Irish envoys were about to join the Egyptians, Boers and Indians in a league of 'victims of empire'. These reports

were soon censored, despite their accuracy, because of apparent alarm on the part of the British intelligence authorities, spooked by anti-colonial discontent thought to be fuelled by the impact of the Bolshevik Revolution in 1917 and Woodrow Wilson's Fourteen Points.

Whatever the ideological driving forces, establishing contacts with fellow anti-imperialists in Paris proved an easier task for the Irish envoys than their primary objective of winning recognition for the Irish Republic. The conference drew to a close without a hearing for the Irish case, let alone admission to the League of Nations. The Egyptians, despite mounting a more successful propaganda campaign than the Irish, were also ultimately unsuccessful in gaining international recognition. Wilson's altruistic Fourteen Points and his small-nation rhetoric were never intended for Ireland or Egypt but rather for the Poles, Finns and Czechs; it was perhaps naïve to have hoped otherwise. But the work in Paris had established an Irish–Egyptian revolutionary network, which was revived in London during the months of negotiations by both countries with the British government in 1921.

In London, contacts between Irish republicans and Egyptians were primarily cultivated by the Irish

envoy there, Art O'Brien, president of the Sinn Féin Council of Great Britain. Two separate Egyptian delegations had been sent to London to negotiate terms of agreement with Britain in the wake of the 1919 revolution. The second arrived in June 1921, at the same time as the 1921 Imperial Conference was taking place; dominion delegates would be privy to the negotiations and would stress the necessity of holding on to control of the Suez Canal. Autumn 1921 was a demanding time for the British government, and Philip Kerr, then personal secretary to the prime minister, was only too cognisant of the possible knock-on effects that dealing with the Egyptians and the Irish in close succession and proximity could have. He warned Liberal Prime Minister David Lloyd George that, if they didn't push for a reasonable settlement, 'Zaghlul will go Sinn Féin, and though we can put him down, Zaghlul will begin to create a Pan-Islamic-Sinn Féin machine making mischief everywhere'.

Mischief-making was already happening under his nose in London. W. Makram Ebeid, who—along with Saad Zaghloul—was a founder member of the Wafd party, had secured an introduction to Art O'Brien from Duffy and Ó Ceallaigh in Paris. He wanted a 'demonstration

● Above: Australian troops at the Pyramids—many soldiers went straight from the battlefields of the Great War to policing the Empire.

of sympathy between the two nations' and, to this end, sought an invitation to Dublin. Ebeid suggested that 'the English Government will regard with dissatisfaction any sign of the two nations seeming to work in a common interest'. O'Brien agreed that collaboration of this kind would be beneficial to both causes. On receipt of an invitation, Ebeid intended to travel over with some dozen or so friends, call on de Valera officially and address as many meetings as possible. Ebeid kept O'Brien up to date with developments and, indeed, provided details of the breakdown of the negotiations for him. This liaison was fortuitous, given that it coincided with the Irish envoys' arrival in London to begin the Anglo-Irish Treaty negotiations. Makram Ebeid wrote detailed letters to O'Brien outlining the moderate

British proposals that would clash with the increasingly radical Egyptian political landscape:

'[Prime Minister] Adly Pasha could not obviously accept these proposals which amounted to a consecration of the Status Quo, both in internal and external matters and the negotiations have failed for that reason. But it is admitted that the crux of the whole problem, was the military occupation of Egypt upon which Curzon and Churchill were adamant.'

Lloyd George, on the other hand, Ebeid told O'Brien, 'realised that the whole country was behind Zaghloul Pasha in the claim for *complete independence* and that the points accepted by Adly would not be accepted by the Egyptian people'. This scenario provided a striking foreshadowing of issues central to the upcoming Anglo-Irish negotiations.

In the meantime, de Valera had responded favourably to Ebeid's

approaches and plans were being put in place to receive an Egyptian delegation in Dublin. It would be headed by Ebeid and Dr Mahmoud, one of Zaghloul Pasha's secretaries. The Egyptians were keen to know whether the press would be informed and to have an itinerary of their trip. O'Brien was asked to consult Arthur Griffith in his capacity as Minister for Foreign Affairs and, more crucially, because he was then in London negotiating with the British government. But de Valera, it seems, was anxious not to ruffle any feathers; he ruled out a public meeting with the delegation, as he was concerned that 'political capital could be made of it', which could be detrimental to the ongoing negotiations. O'Brien was told by Dublin that 'the 8th of December will be a suitable date for them to be received by the President at the Mansion House'. They were to be met by Patrick McCartan and 'shown every courtesy and attention. A formal luncheon or dinner will be arranged to which will be invited such well-known Irishmen as A.E., Count Plunkett, James Stevens, Dr Gogerty [sic] and others.' The Egyptian delegation was due to set sail on the morning of 7 December but never did. It turned out to be the least suitable of dates: the Anglo-Irish Treaty of 1921 had been signed the previous day, plunging the country into a state of disarray and confusion.

New perspectives can emerge from well-trodden avenues of history. The story of Irish republican connections with Egyptian activists in London was eclipsed by the more dramatic political events that followed the signing of the Treaty in December 1921. As is explored in Kenneth Shonk's essay, there were many other instances where Ireland's influence was evident as the decolonisation process gained momentum in the mid-twentieth century. There are also examples of the Irish revolution having influenced anti-colonialist leaders such as the Gold Coast nationalist revolutionary Kwame Nkrumah, who cited Ireland as a source of inspiration and asked for a copy of Patrick Pearse's collected works when he visited Dublin after becoming the first president of Ghana in 1960. Similarly, Algerian nationalists struggling under French rule in the 1950s approached Irish representatives at the United Nations in New York. They were particularly keen to learn about the negotiations that led to the Anglo-Irish Truce of 1921. Elsewhere in Asia, the Irish minister in Australia, Thomas J. Kiernan, met Ali Sastroamidjojo (later Indonesian prime minister) in the 1940s. Having read Dan Breen's *My fight for Irish freedom*, Indonesian insurgents were seeking further information on guerrilla warfare in pursuit of their struggle against Dutch forces in Indonesia.

Finally, and more generally, great efforts were made by the British intelligence authorities to monitor the many anti-imperialist connections established during the interwar period. And we should be grateful: their fastidiousness often made them the best chroniclers of

their own revolutionary enemies. It could be argued, though, that the British government failed to see the wood for the trees during these years. In 1919 the authorities initially perceived these events as merely hitches in the imperial sphere, and attempted to keep anti-imperialists at bay via 'intra-imperial' negotiations. Taking a step back from events in Dublin or Cairo in 1919, however, it can be seen that these episodes were clearly crucial moments on the peripheries which both prefaced and beckoned the unavoidable course of the demise of the British Empire.

Kate O'Malley is a historian with the Royal Irish Academy and author of *Ireland, India and Empire: Indo-Irish radical connections, 1919–64 (Manchester, 2008).*

Further reading

N.I. Khan, *Egyptian–Indian nationalist collaboration and the British Empire* (London, 2011).

E. Manela, *The Wilsonian moment: self-determination and the international origins of anticolonial nationalism* (Oxford, 2007).

Below: Dan Breen—Indian and Indonesian revolutionaries were influenced by his book, *My fight for Irish freedom.* (Kilmainham Gaol)

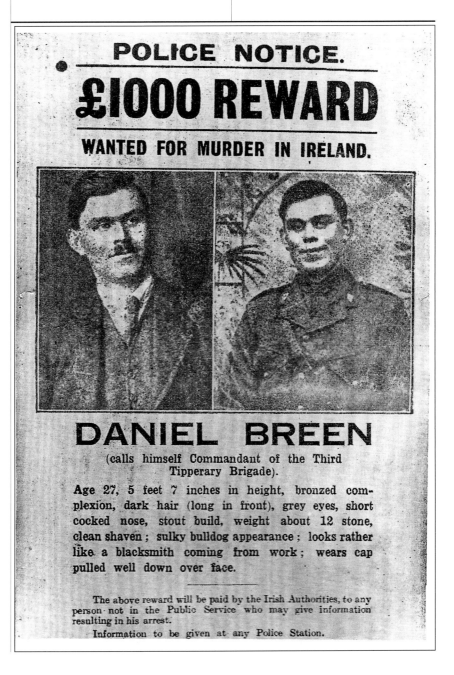

POLICE NOTICE.

£1000 REWARD

WANTED FOR MURDER IN IRELAND.

DANIEL BREEN

(calls himself Commandant of the Third Tipperary Brigade).

Age 27, 5 feet 7 inches in height, bronzed complexion, dark hair (long in front), grey eyes, short cocked nose, stout build, weight about 12 stone, clean shaven; sulky bulldog appearance; looks rather like a blacksmith coming from work; wears cap pulled well down over face.

The above reward will be paid by the Irish Authorities, to any person not in the Public Service who may give information resulting in his arrest.
Information to be given at any Police Station.

THE SHADOW METROPOLIS:

GLOBAL ANTI-COLONIALISM AND THE LEGACY OF IRELAND'S REVOLUTION

BY **KENNETH SHONK**

etween 1937 and 1968 a large number of anti-colonial nationalists from myriad nations throughout Asia, Africa, Europe and the Americas visited Dublin. Both in public and in private they expressed their admiration for the actions and achievements of Irish leaders, whom they clearly sought to emulate. Among them were seminal figures who would play a central role in the process of global decolonisation during these pivotal decades. They came to pay their respects to the founders of the Irish state, most notably Éamon de Valera, but also to align their own liberation movements with Ireland by seeking validation and support from Irish nationalist politicians who during this period were successfully dissolving Ireland's place within, first, the Union and, subsequently, the Empire and Commonwealth. These nationalist activists and intellectuals sought also to convey an understanding of—and kinship with—a reading of history whereby the achievements of Irish nationalists were seen as central to the wider progress achieved by twentieth-century anti-colonial nationalists.

Utilised as a space—both real and imagined—that allowed various global nationalist movements to negotiate their entry into the realm of the newly free, Dublin can be seen as a 'shadow metropolis': a counter, or inversion, of the imperial centres of empire in London, Paris or Brussels. Global familiarity with Ireland's history of rebellion and revolution bequeathed to the independent Irish state a symbolic role and status as an anti-colonial bulwark. At the same time, though, the desire of anti-colonial nationalists to emulate Ireland was increasingly at odds with how the Irish state was choosing to frame its own international political identity.

Speaking before the International Study Congress in Dublin on 26 June 1960, Taoiseach Seán Lemass situated Ireland as a nation willing to assist—but not lead—developing nations. His language had echoes of paternalism, distancing Ireland from the radical liberation narratives identified above. The taoiseach, for example, began by asking: 'To what extent and in what manner can a small country like Ireland make a worthwhile contribution to the world problem?' Lemass acknowledged that any financial contribution by Ireland would 'be a mere drop in the ocean', yet Ireland, he suggested, could aid developing nations seeking to overcome 'administrative handicaps' by offering advice. This aspiration to assist developing nations was borne out by many of the actions undertaken by the Irish government in the 1950s and 1960s. It was evident, for example, in the Irish government's willingness to provide guidance by way of past domestic initiatives to leaders from Sudan (on parliamentarianism), Tanganyika (housing) and Nigeria (education), among many other developing states.

On the surface, then, it might appear that Ireland was willing to acknowledge its importance to developing nations in Africa and Asia, as well as Soviet Bloc nations. Yet a closer analysis of Lemass's speech reveals a rhetoric that situates Ireland as the more powerful, European provider: that is, a saviour of sorts. First, Lemass sought to reiterate Ireland's 'Europeanness' by stating that the 'small, progressive nations of Western Europe, amongst which we count our own, can give a very useful helping hand to those countries now struggling to nationhood'. The paternalism of this statement is evident, and is equally apparent in Lemass's offer to provide these nations with 'technical aid and advice'.

Right: Two Victor Weisz cartoons that appeared in the *Evening Standard* in the early 1960s. In 'H.M. SCHOOL FOR PRIME MINISTERS' (above right), de Valera is among the former occupants of the prison from which Kenya's Jomo Kenyatta has been released; and (right) Malawi's Hastings Banda occupies a cell that held other revolutionaries, among them de Valera. (British Cartoon Archive)

Opposite page: Éamon de Valera in Wisconsin, 18 October 1919, where he was made an honorary chief of the Chippewa nation. The Irish leader proved an enduring inspiration for colonial peoples. (UCD Archives)

For their part, however, the discourse of leaders from these 'less advanced overseas countries' made clear that they were influenced by a shared history of sorts centring on a common tradition of anti-imperialist struggle. For example, when Dr Mahmoud Fawzi—Foreign Minister

Above: Kwame Nkrumah and Jawaharlal Nehru at Downing Street in 1957. Visiting Dublin three years later, Nkrumah described how he and de Valera were both 'prison graduates'. (Alamy)

of Egypt—visited Dublin in 1960, he expressed his admiration for 'Ireland's great struggle for liberty and her attachment to high ideals of humanity and loyalty to principles which she had proved over and over again'. Visiting Dublin in the same year, Kwame Nkrumah, the Ghanaian revolutionary, posited a similar if more radical political parallel, noting that he and de Valera had gone to the 'same college': 'we are both prison graduates'.

Two remarkable political cartoons from the 1960s, by *Evening Standard* cartoonist Victor Weisz, reinforced this idea of a shared anti-imperialist history by depicting de Valera as the first of a relatively long list of successful anti-colonial leaders who had been 'educated' in British prisons. In the first, the Kenyan independence leader Jomo Kenyatta is depicted leaving a prison dubbed 'The H.M. School for Prime Ministers'. To his right is a sign depicting those that have 'stayed here'. De Valera, listed first, is followed by Nehru (India), Nkrumah (Ghana), Banda

(Malawi), Makarios (Cyprus), Jagan (Guyana) and Kenyatta. In the second, Hastings Banda, the president of Malawi, is depicted in a dream bubble of sorts, sitting tieless in prison. Written on the prison cell's wall are the names of previous occupants—Nehru, Nkrumah, Jagan and Makarios. Listed first, above them all, is de Valera.

In his speech, however, Lemass—a revolutionary contemporary of de Valera's—seemed to wilfully ignore this shared colonial history, instead insisting that overseas familiarity with Ireland was the result of the country's 'substantial contribution to the progress of less advanced overseas countries' by way of 'our missionary movement overseas'. Indeed, there was a very strong presence of Irish missionaries throughout the world, by which many thousands were educated through a curriculum that included the Gospels and tracts on Irish nationhood. Yet Lemass presented this relationship as paternalistic in depicting the Irish as contributing to these less advanced nations' progress toward development and independence, rather than sharing a similar historical trajectory. In this regard, Lemass seemed to be willing to overlook Ireland's anti-imperialist

history for the sake of distancing Ireland from the non-European other. He went on to claim, remarkably, that Ireland's 'record is, for instance, free from any taint of imperialism or colonialism', and to offer to 'help [other nations] in organising their public services'.

On its own, Lemass's speech might be disregarded as an isolated case—perhaps even a prudent stance, given the wider Cold War context that saw anti-colonial revolutionaries identified with communism. Yet two major points suggest otherwise. First, Lemass was far from alone in expressing these sentiments; numerous other Irish politicians and intellectuals echoed similar thoughts. Second was Ireland's hesitancy to undertake a position of leadership within the nascent efforts to unite the Non-Aligned nations. Why did Ireland not take a position of international leadership amongst the anti-colonial (or, later, the Non-Aligned) states?

The possibility was certainly suggested to them. In September 1958, a delegation of African diplomats visited Ireland as part of a European tour intended to gain support for the cause of Algerian independence. In addition to making statements heralding Ireland's anti-colonial past and its 'love of freedom', A. Abdelalae of Morocco stated that 'Mr de Valera was the inspiration of African Nationalists'. A clear demonstration of public support for Algerian independence would have firmly placed Ireland within the cause of the Non-Aligned states. To do so, however, would have run counter to Ireland's burgeoning desire to secure membership of the European Economic Community. Consequently, the Irish government refused to offer its support to this radical cause.

A further example of Ireland serving as the physical locus of a shadow metropolis is evident in Burma's 1947–8 constitutional mission to Ireland, led by U Chan Htoon. During October and November 1947 the constitutional adviser to the government of Burma visited Ireland 'to see how the [Irish]

Constitution worked in practice'. The 1 November 1947 edition of the *Irish Press* contained the following passage:

'Mr de Valera, whom [Htoon] saw on Thursday, was as well-known in Burma as in Ireland, and the strategy of the nationalist parties in Burma had been largely based on the republican movement in Ireland since 1916 … The examples of the Lord Mayor of Cork, Terence MacSwiney, had been followed in 1924 in Burma by U Wismarah, the nationalist leader of the time, who had died after 124 days on hunger strike.'

The report concluded with the following quote from U Chan Htoon: 'The fact that we patterned our Constitution on yours is the greatest tribute we could pay to your country'. U Maung Maung, another member of the delegation, added later that 'The constitution of the Republic of Ireland was also frequently consulted for inspiration and guidance'. A cursory read of the 1948 Burmese constitution reveals fundamental similarities with the 1937 Irish constitution, primarily in matters of citizenship, the elevation into primacy of an officially recognised religion (Buddhism), and concerning the transference and ownership of land.

An international awareness of Irish history was a key facet permitting Ireland's emergence as a shadow metropolis. The period could be seen as beginning in 1937, a significant year in terms of Irish efforts to cut its Commonwealth ties, when Korean composer and nationalist Eak Tai Ahn chose to debut his patriotic song *Aegugka*—now South Korea's national anthem—in Dublin to what he viewed as a most sympathetic and understanding audience. For Eak Tai, the Ireland of the 1930s represented a model of what Korea might become: a small nation that had successfully broken free of its colonial ties to become independent.

Ireland's recent history held great importance for anti-colonial politicians who aspired to national independence during these mid-twentieth-century decades marked by the Cold War and the collapse of western imperial frameworks. Interestingly, the history remarked upon by these nationalist leaders was not the Ireland of Tone, Davis, Parnell or of the insurrectionary republicanism of Pearse and Connolly; nor were they keen to forge anew the sorts of transnational partnerships detailed in Kate O'Malley's essay. Instead, it was the political manoeuvrings undertaken in de Valera's Ireland during the 1930s and 1940s that resonated most, as such endeavours were deemed more likely to succeed in the imperial realignment that followed the end of the Second World War. As U Thant, the Burmese nationalist politician (and then UN secretary general), declared on arrival at Dublin airport during his visit to Ireland in 1962: 'I am particularly gratified at the prospect of paying my visit to your very great President who has been a source of inspiration to the people in my part of the world who, in those days, were struggling for freedom'.

The examples detailed in this essay add greater nuance to our understanding of how the Irish government perceived geopolitical trends, and the extent to which it was willing to engage with global anti-colonialists who not only sought political ties with Ireland but also sought to elevate Ireland as a model for nationalist progress. Ireland's status as a shadow metropolis demonstrates how, during these decades, numerous anti-colonial politicians throughout the world looked towards Ireland as a significant actor in the global story of anti-imperial struggle. As the Ghanaian nationalist Kwame Nkrumah noted in 1960: 'the struggle for Ireland for independence was not the struggle of one country alone, but part of a world movement for freedom … In its essence the problem of Africa today reproduces the problem of Ireland of yesterday.' The following year, Nyasaland (later Malawi) nationalist Hastings Banda similarly claimed that 'The history of Ireland is a worthy history and her fight for independence is an inspiration to

any country yearning to be free'.

Ireland's negotiated withdrawal from the British Empire and Commonwealth represented a touchstone for anti-colonial nations seeking an emulative model by which to attain independence and foster nascent structures of nation-building. Ironically, however, this occurred just as Ireland was recasting itself as a state firmly dedicated to pursuing membership of the burgeoning European Economic community. Consequently, there was a divergence of interpretation concerning Ireland's recent history: for the Irish, it was the story of a European nation emerging triumphantly from imperial rule. For African and Asian anti-colonial nationalists, recent events in Ireland were seminal in global history for heralding the onset of the decline and fall of European colonialism. For Nkrumah, Fawzi, U Thant and Banda, among others, Ireland's global importance was without question.

Kenneth Shonk Jr teaches history at the University of Wisconsin-La Crosse.

Further reading

P.L. Wylie, *Ireland and the Cold War, diplomacy and recognition, 1949–1963* (Dublin, 2006).

●

Above: Indian nationalist and later ambassador to Ireland Vijaya Lakshmi ('Madame') Pandit. In 1955 she told how she was 'thrilled by the Irish Rising in 1916 and have stayed thrilled by Ireland's story ever since'. (NPG)

HUNGER STRIKING BEYOND IRELAND: THE GLOBAL CONTEXT

BY **IAN MILLER**

The hunger strikes of Thomas Ashe (1917) and Terence MacSwiney (1920) are remembered as pivotal moments of the Irish Revolution. It is often forgotten, however, that hundreds of Irish prisoners also went on hunger strike during both the War of Independence and the Civil War. In addition, a lasting interest in Irish hunger striking often draws attention away from the fact that prisoners, mostly politicised, continued to hunger strike globally long after the tumultuous events of the Irish Revolution had drawn to a close. Indeed, one historian has described the period between the 1910s and 1940s as a 'golden age of the hunger strike in anti-colonial struggles'. Across the globe, in places as diverse as India, Israel and South Africa, politicised prisoners and detainees protested simply by refusing to eat, taking influence from earlier Irish hunger strikers and leaving various governments in a difficult position. Yet if the hunger strike itself was exported from Britain and Ireland, where suffragettes had pioneered the strategy in the years before the First World War, so too were the various practices and procedures used by governments to defeat them, most notably force-feeding. Prison deaths were to be avoided at all costs, but releasing or force-feeding hunger strikers against their wishes were equally undesirable options.

India provided a major colonial context in which nationalists, as in Ireland, used hunger striking to challenge the legitimacy of British rule during periods of political agitation. In the 1910s, a turn to militancy within Indian nationalism increased the numbers of politicised prisoners. From the 1920s, participants in the non-violent Non-Cooperation Movement staged less-confrontational hunger strikes. The 1930s, however, saw an upsurge of revolutionary violence and more aggressive hunger striking, encouraging the government to standardise the use of force-feeding across Indian prisons. The granting of Indian independence (and partition) in 1947 brought an end to this period of hunger striking.

Just as Terence MacSwiney, the former lord mayor of Cork, looms large as a key Irish hunger striker, Mahatma Gandhi is the best-remembered Indian hunger striker. Between 1914 and 1948 Gandhi pursued fifteen internationally reported hunger strikes, but thousands of lesser-known and overshadowed men and women also refused food in India. As in revolutionary Ireland, hunger striking was not pursued only by a few determined individuals but instead became a deeply embedded practice used widely to protest harsh prison conditions and political injustice. Between the 1910s and 1940s, Indian hunger striking was remarkably common and geographically widespread. Major group hunger strikes took place in Mandalay (1929), Delhi (1930), Andamans (1930s), Alipore (1937), Berhampore (1937) and many other places. As in Ireland, prisons were a key site in which colonial power could be exerted (directly onto the body in the case of force-feeding) but also actively resisted.

During 1920 the Indian press reported widely on MacSwiney's

ENGLAND'S LATEST VICTIMS

JATINDRANATH DAS, Indian Nationalist leader has died after 61 days' hunger strike in Lahore British Jail.

A Buddhist Monk has also died after 63 days' Hunger Strike. They have been slowly murdered by order of the British Government because they taught the doctrine of India for the Indians.

Their names shall be remembered for ever with THOMAS ASHE, TERENCE Mac SWEENEY, TAIDHG O'SULLIVAN, DINNY BARRY, MICHAEL FITZGERALD and J. MURPHY.

Speaking at the funeral of Jatindranath Das, the major of Calcutta urged the people to refuse to recognise British law in India, and to be ready to choose prison and death rather than accept the tolerance accorded to slaves.

Again, in a recent leaflet hurled with bombs at the Ministers in the so-called Indian parliament, the representatives of the people were asked to return to their constituencies and prepare the masses for the coming Revolution.

The Indian Republican Army is arming and organising for the coming Revolution Shall we in Ireland leave India to fight alone?

As India depends on her Army to deliver her from British rule, so Ireland depends on the Irish Republican Army to overthrow the two British-imposed governments at present operating by force.

Are we giving the support they deserve to this patriotic band of Volunteers?

The greatest monument we can erect to the memory of these martyred Hunger-Strikers is the overthrowal of British rule in Ireland.

Hasten the Revolution by supporting the Irish Republican Army, Cumann na mBan and Sinn Fein.

Issued by Cumann na mBan.

hunger strike and subsequent death, bringing Indian nationalists into contact with the idea of refusing food as protest. By the end of the decade, Indians could claim to have their very own MacSwiney. In 1929 Jatindra Nath Das, a Bengal-based revolutionary, died after a 63-day hunger strike. Arrested in June 1929 for revolutionary activities and imprisoned in Lahore Jail, he went on hunger strike to demand equality for Indian political prisoners with those from Europe. Unlike in the case of MacSwiney, prison officials tried to force-feed him. When this failed, they recommended early release. The colonial government, however, refused to give in to Das, who eventually died on 13 September 1929. His plight attracted considerable sympathy. He became known as the 'Indian Terence MacSwiney', and his family received letters of support and sympathy from the late mayor of Cork's family.

●
Above right: A Cumann na mBan leaflet applauds the sacrifice of Jatindranath Das (above), a Bengal-based revolutionary who died after a 63-day hunger strike in 1929. Das became known as the 'Indian Terence MacSwiney'. (NLI)

●
Opposite page: A rally to welcome Muriel MacSwiney, widow of Terence, at West Street, Manhattan, on 4 December 1920. The MacSwiney hunger strike had a huge impact on American opinion.

Nevertheless, it would be wrong to view Indian hunger striking simply as an extension of Irish practices. In a country as large and diverse as India, regional and cultural differences inevitably existed. Indian protestors had to adapt hunger striking to suit their own political and cultural agendas and practices. Notably, Gandhi felt ill at ease with the violence of the Irish revolution and physical-force approaches. Irish revolutionaries had certainly inspired him to adopt the hunger strike, but he sought to incorporate the strategy into his non-violent philosophies. The peaceful Gandhian hunger strike could not encompass prison rioting or attacks on doctors who attempted force-feeding.

Violence was, however, undoubtedly far more crucial to other Indian nationalist groups, particularly those in militant areas. Bengali nationalists openly admired Ireland's violent resistance of British rule and incorporated physical force into their own approaches. They used hunger striking in far more confrontational ways than other Indian nationalists. Leaders such as Subhas Chandra Bose looked directly to Ireland as a heroic model of anti-colonial resistance and as a blueprint for Indian national liberation. Of course, this perspective overlooked the problematic issue of partition (a fate to which India also found itself violently subjected in 1947), as well as the fact that Ireland had not been entirely liberated. Despite these issues, many Indian nationalists pointed to Ireland as the first example of a successful, if not quite complete, rebellion against British rule.

As the twentieth century unfolded, the Irish republican hunger strikes of the 1910s and 1920s seemed increasingly distant. While they no longer provided an immediate influence on other protestors (at least until Northern Irish republicans resumed hunger striking between 1980 and 1981), the Irish had undoubtedly helped establish hunger striking as a standard protest against political and institutional injustice. Unlike in the 1910s, when the suffragettes developed the use of hunger striking as political protest, the vast majority of hunger strikers, although by no means all, were male (reflecting the higher number of male prisoners). Israel provides one example. Since Israel's 1967 occupation of the West Bank, East Jerusalem and the Gaza

●

Below: The H-Block hunger strikes of 1980–1 renewed global interest in the use of this tactic by Irish republican prisoners.

Strip, Palestinians have launched numerous solitary and group hunger strikes. In some cases prisoners successfully negotiated with the authorities to improve conditions, but other hunger strikers were placed in solitary confinement or had family visits withheld. As in Ireland and India, some of these hunger strikes were remarkably extensive. In 1984 over 800 prisoners joined a hunger strike aiming to secure better conditions in Nablus prison. In 1987 over 3,000 prisoners participated in a nationwide hunger strike, while over 7,000 prisoners went on hunger strike during the 1992 elections.

South Africa also witnessed numerous hunger strikes during the Apartheid period (1948–94). Prisoners held in institutions such as Robben Island came from diverse political backgrounds, including the African National Congress, the Pan African Congress, and black consciousness and communist movements. For group hunger strikes to

be effective, prisoners needed to overcome their political differences and protest together to improve their institutional conditions or to gain political status. In many ways, hunger striking helped to bring diverse individuals together. As in revolutionary Ireland, *en masse* hunger strikes proved most effective in achieving their aims.

In 1966 almost the entire prison population of Robben Island, around 1,000 men, went on hunger strike. During the 1980s numerous hunger strikes took place at Robben Island, some of which were widely supported by the majority of prisoners while others had only the support of smaller groups. In February 1989, however, about 800 detainees began a co-ordinated nationwide hunger strike that forced the government to consider releasing them. In 1990 President F.W. de Klerk announced that Nelson Mandela and other prisoners were to be released, although the govern-

ment did not seem to be in a hurry to authorise these releases. Release was accelerated by various group hunger strikes across the South African prison system.

Alongside the idea of hunger striking itself, the use of force-feeding to tackle hunger strikes is an important legacy of the 1910s. Just as hunger strikes were exported globally from Britain and Ireland, colonial governments exported their techniques for crushing institutional protest. Force-feeding involves inserting a nasal or stomach tube into a prisoner, usually against his or her will. The passing of the tube caused most prisoners to gag, choke and vomit. A prison doctor would then pour liquid food into the tube. Most force-fed prisoners insisted that the procedure was used primarily to punish, degrade and harm. They claimed that the passing of a stomach tube through the inner body was intensely painful, as well as emotionally traumatic. Force-feeding was also known to kill when a doctor accidentally poured liquid food into the lungs rather than the stomach, causing a rapid, unpleasant death from pneumonia.

The suffragettes, between 1909 and 1914, were the first group of hunger strikers to be force-fed by the British government. The adoption of force-feeding, a procedure that had only been used previously in asylums, caused considerable public outrage. Nonetheless, the government claimed that it was the only way to save the lives of 'suicidal' women. In Ireland a small number of suffragettes were force-fed, alongside trade unionists around the time of the Dublin Lockout. During 1917, republicans in prisons such as Mountjoy went on hunger strike and were also force-fed. Notoriously, Thomas Ashe died from heart problems seemingly brought on by his force-feeding. The death of Ashe, a key leader of the Easter Rising outside of Dublin, caused a major public outcry. His funeral procession lined the streets of Dublin; Michael Collins gave a short but powerful oration.

The government mostly aban-doned force-feeding in Ireland after Ashe's death, but only because of a fear of inflaming the country's tense political situation even further. Despite this high-profile death and irrefutable proof of the potential danger of force-feeding, the authorities exhibited little concern about the procedure's ethical implications or its potential to be used as a punitive instrument. As in revolutionary Ireland, governments internationally were forced to grapple with the question of whether hunger strikers should be force-fed, as Ashe had been, or left to starve, like MacSwiney. In reality, the vast majority of Irish hunger strikers had been prematurely released after around fifteen days of not eating. This, however, was not always a feasible option in other sites of twentieth-century conflict.

Since the 1960s the Israeli government has regularly force-fed hunger strikers, sometimes causing death. In 1970 Abdul Qader Abu Al-Fahm became the first Palestinian prisoner to die during hunger strike, when a stomach tube accidentally slipped into his lungs rather than his stomach. In 1980 Rasem Halawah and Ali Jafari both died from the effects of force-feeding in Nafa Prison. Regardless of its dangerous potential, both hunger striking and force-feeding remain a fixture of Israeli prison life. Force-feeding has also been widely used in other countries, including South Africa, Turkey and, more recently, at Guantanamo Bay, where hundreds of detainees have chosen to protest against their detention by hunger striking.

Clearly, political responses to hunger strikes varied in different contexts. Force-feeding may not have been a viable political response in revolutionary Ireland, but it persisted as a central feature of hunger strike experiences when prisoners across the globe refused food in the century following the Irish War of Independence and the Civil War. It was only in 1975 that the World Medical Association's Ethics Committee finally declared force-feeding unethical following the deaths of a number of IRA prisoners

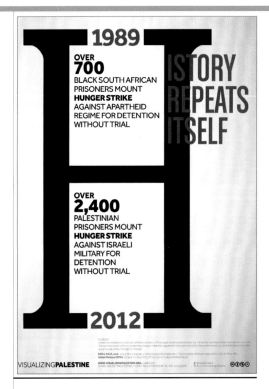

in Britain, where the practice was still legal. While not all countries adhered to these new guidelines, the British and Northern Irish governments did, explaining in part why force-feeding was considered an inappropriate option during the infamous 1980–1 Maze/Long Kesh hunger strikes in which ten Irish republicans died in the face of British Prime Minister Margaret Thatcher's refusal to grant political status to republican prisoners.

Ian Miller lectures in British and Irish history at Ulster University and co-curated a museum exhibition at Kilmainham Gaol on hunger strike history as part of the Decade of Centenaries programme.

Further reading

F.L. Buntman, *Robben Island and prisoner resistance to apartheid* (Cambridge, 2004).

I. Miller, *A history of force feeding: hunger strikes, prisons and medical ethics, 1909–1974* (London, 2016).

U.K. Singh, *Political prisoners in India* (New Delhi, 2001).

●

Above: Since the 1960s hunger striking has been utilised on several occasions by political prisoners in South Africa and Palestine.

CULTURAL CURRENTS

Mobilise the poets. Let them address Wilson, and let them remind him in their best verse that he has the opportunity and the duty of giving the world true peace and freedom. Let them exhort him to stand firm and win a greater victory for man than any that has been won for centuries.

—Arthur Griffith, TD and Sinn Féin vice-president, Gloucester Prison, 23 January 1919

Image: IRA prisoners in Ballykinlar, Co. Down, formed a fiddle band, playing concerts which included 'selections of Irish music' and providing the music for a *céilidh* to mark Labour Day in 1921. (Kilmainham Gaol)

THE 'EMBASSADRESS' FROM ELFLAND: ELLA YOUNG AND THE GLOBAL REVOLUTION

BY **LAUREN ARRINGTON**

Left: Ella Young, described as an 'Embassadress' from 'Elfland' on her arrival in the US during 1925.

'Elfland sends an Embassadress to us': so began an article in the *New York Times Sunday Supplement* announcing the arrival of Ella Young in the United States in the autumn of 1925. By the time she emigrated, Young had established herself in Ireland as a prolific poet, a strident republican and a frequent collaborator with Maud Gonne. Despite her prominence in cultural revivalist movements in Ireland, she was relatively unfamiliar to an American audience. Her reputation in the US grew under the direction of a shrewd publicist and blossomed with the publication—by Longmans, Greene and Co. in 1927—of *The Wonder Smith and his son*, one of her fantastical and pedagogical tales for children. *The Wonder Smith* was illustrated by the Russian émigré Boris Artzybasheff, who eventually eclipsed Young in fame owing to his acclaimed surrealist drawings, which featured repeatedly on the covers of *Time*, *Fortune* and *Life* magazines. Young's work with Artzybasheff marks one intersection between revolutionary politics and the modernist revolution in the visual arts, and her text and his drawings demonstrate the global ideas at play in both.

During the Celtic Revival, Young's writing revisited origin myths in order to advocate a feminist philosophy, giving prominence to female iterations of powerful spiritual and military leaders, both real and imagined. Her work conjoined gender and mysticism in a way that is similar to the poems and plays of Eva Gore-Booth. Whereas Gore-Booth was a pacifist advocate of Irish independence, however, Young's idiosyncratic spirituality inspired poems that aestheticised violence. She went so far as to believe that her writing was a major aspect of her engagement 'in the battle for Irish sovereignty'. Scholar Aurelia Annat writes that 'for Young, a battle waged on cultural and mystical terms was as important as one with guns'.

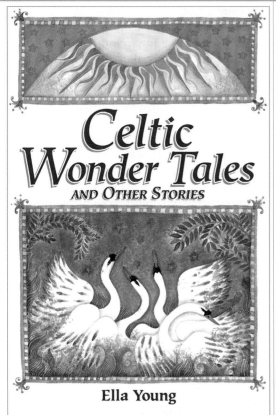

Ella Young

Like many republican women in the 1920s, when Young sailed from Queenstown (Cobh), Co. Cork, for New York it was with the inten-

Top: Young's first story collection, *Celtic wonder tales and other stories* (1910), was illustrated by Maud Gonne McBride (above).

tion of undertaking a lecture tour of the United States. Documents recovered by Dorothea McDowell in *Ella Young and her world* (2014) show how the American authorities were unconvinced about the purpose of Young's visit and initially denied her entry, suspecting that she was 'a probable mental case when they learned that she believed in the existence of fairies, elves and pixies'. Immigration officials raised further questions owing to Young's age and indigence: 58 years old with no guaranteed income. Through the support of Gavin Arthur, grandson of the largely forgotten 21st president of the United States, Young was admitted to the country on a temporary permit, and what had been a cause of suspicion became a cause of celebration. The *New York Times* declared: 'Her most surprising gift—and one that will endear her to all Americans with whom she comes in contact while lecturing here—is a privilege of access to the haunts and ways of fairies [...] Children in the Wild West of Ireland have recounted to her their dealings with eery playmates of the woods and fields; of spell-weaving lullabies bringing slumber.'

On her arrival in New York, Young was under the 'exclusive management' of the William B. Feakins publicity company, which also represented other politically prominent women on lecture tours, including the humanitarian activist Lady Muriel Paget and 'Red Ellen' Wilkinson, co-founder of the British Communist Party. Feakins's agency pinched the title of a chapter from *Peter Pan* for its advertisements of Young's talks: 'Do You Believe in Fairies? Ella Young knows all about the fairies and fairy doings'. It was a clever move, capitalising on audiences who had been captivated by the silent film released by Paramount in late 1924 and starring—in the role of Peter—Betty Bronson, who would later play alongside Jack Benny. The film began with a caveat that very much reflected Young's own world-view: 'The difference between a Fairy Play and a realistic one is that in the

former all the characters are really children with a child's outlook on life. This applies to the so-called adults of the story as well as the young people.' Young believed that her stories were for children of all ages, but she found that actual children were the most receptive—and very young children, at that. When she arrived at a Catholic academy in California, expecting to lecture on Greek, Norse and 'Celtic' versions of Fate to older teenagers, she discovered that her audience consisted of the academy's littlest pupils. Young quickly and adroitly recalibrated and regaled the group with adventure lore, which was her real strength anyhow.

In the early years of the Celtic Revival, Young was very active in the Daughters of Ireland (Inghinidhe na hÉireann) and, later, in Cumann na mBan. A significant aspect of her role in the former was to teach 'history' through telling 'sagas and hero-tales' to impoverished children in Dublin. This experience led to her ambition to publish stories that would be accessible to younger readers—and it also brought about her association with Gonne, who was an early illustrator of her books. Much like the poems themselves, Young and Gonne's collaborations were a mixed bag; *The rose of heaven* (1920), their last book, blends Rosicrucian imagery, medieval French, old Irish and ancient Greek tropes, and is written for an élite, adult readership capable of decoding the complex symbolism amid the uneven verse.

During the same period, Young had a more direct involvement in the republican struggle. She helped distribute the Irish Volunteers' rifles landed at Howth in 1914, was involved in preparations for the Easter Rising and supported Cumann na mBan's military campaign during the War of Independence. Like many within Cumann na mBan, she took the anti-Treaty side during the Civil War. After the Civil War, she was among a group of republicans that congregated around Gonne, deeming themselves 'the Optimists'.

The positivist republican vision articulated by the group's name reflects Young's broader philosophy as a mystic. Especially after she moved to the United States, her spiritualism and Irish republicanism found expression—and perhaps personal justification—in her construction of a global mythology of which Irish stories formed just one part.

Young's first American book, *The Wonder Smith and his son*, was subtitled *A tale from the golden childhood of the world*. Her foreword identifies the smith of the title as 'The Gubbaun Saor, whose other name was Mananaun, whose other name was Cullion the Smith [...] He was a maker of worlds and a shaper of universes. Men said the stars were sparks from his anvil.' Young's repeated description of the Gubbaun as 'Master-Builder' and 'Master-Craftsman' and the recurring image of the anvil evoke tales from Norse mythology, but this is just one of the traditions from which she drew. When the Gubbaun and his son travel to the country of the one-eyed villain Balor, a desert described as a 'hard bleak desolate wilderness', Balor challenges the hero to build a dune 'strong as the foundations of the earth [...] such a dune as never from the beginning of days shaped itself on the ridge of the world'. The Gubbaun rises to the occasion with assistance from mythological creatures from several specific world traditions, including Arabic 'djinns', as well as more universal figures of 'dwarfs, and giants, and goat-footed men, and demons of the air, and fabulous animals, and monstrous beings, and strange beasts'. When Artzybasheff illustrated passages such as this one, he also borrowed from identifiable traditions of sculptural and pictorial representation, including Celtic knotwork but extending to Hindu representations of the snouted elephant god Ganesh and the human-bird and human-horse kinnaras common in India and south-east Asia.

Young was not the only writer from the Celtic Revival who used global mythological sources. Most notably, W.B. Yeats established par-

allels and sometimes integrated Irish mythology with other traditions. Yet what is unusual in Young's work is that her integrated approach to mythology persisted well into the revolutionary period. Furthermore, Yeats imagined the ocean as a medium for accessing another spiritual realm (as in his long poem *The wanderings of Oisin*). By contrast, Young figures the same expanse of water as a conduit for a supposed spiritual connection between Ireland—where, she argues, a particular cultural memory began—and the United States, where the old stories are reinvigorated and then returned to their point of origin. She writes in her foreword:

'In County Clare, huddled between a stony mountain and a boulder-strewn beach where the Atlantic surges leap with a playful roar to the land after their long sea-run from America, there is a little Gaelic-speaking village. Its houses are small and low-roofed, so that storm-winds cannot get too firm a grip on them, and their yellow straw thatch is roped down and weighted with stones to keep the wind from shouldering it away. The people of that village know many stories of the Gubbaun.'

●

Above: Young's work conjoined gender and mysticism in a way that is similar to the poems and plays of Eva Gore-Booth, here painted by her sister Constance. (Lissadell Collection)

Above: One of Russian émigré Boris Artzybasheff's images in Young's *The Wonder Smith and his son* (1927).

She depicts the landscape, the built environment and the people of the west of Ireland as resistant to transient, fickle forces. Her presentation of Irish resilience is obliquely instructive rather than didactic, and her imagery resonates with an American mythology rooted in the natural world:

> 'I am revising these stories for publication in a country that is all delicate pale gold, and the ghost of pale gold, and tawny orange and bronze and amber and russet colour, wherever it is not ermined with snow. A country strong and subtle and graceful as her own mountain lions and cypress trees.'

Young's introduction to *The Wonder Smith* sets the scene for a book that will reflect a romantic enchantment with nature. Instead, readers' expectations are disturbed by Artzybasheff's double-page plates of proto-cyborgs and hybrid human-animal shape-changers.

The collaboration of author and illustrator in *The Wonder Smith* troubles an opposition that critics often draw between romantic enchantment with the natural world and early twentieth-century machine culture, which was positively reflected in the 'efficient' style of some modernist poetry and prose. Whereas Young is firmly placed in the former category, the juxtaposition of literary and pictorial style in *The Wonder Smith* creates an unusual book that is weighted in favour of Young's mystical vision while also giving space to Artzybasheff's experiments with non-human hybrid forms.

Artzybasheff was frequently quoted as saying 'I like machines', but in *The Wonder Smith* machine characteristics are given to the 'baddies', such as Balor's 'dark lords', who wear sharp-featured masks and heavy amour that defines rather than decorates their bodies. Contrastingly, the Gubbaun and his daughter Aunya are depicted as fully human and wholly in control of the world around them. This is important because Young's fantastical plot is an analogy for her republicanism. Despite the central role played by culture in the making of the Irish

Revolution, Young—like many writers and artists who participated in the revival—was ultimately disappointed by the limits of the political revolution. As Annat writes, Young believed that 'the revolution had to be effected metaphysically before it could be enacted physically'. Annat quotes from a letter that Young wrote to the poet Joseph Campbell in 1922, just days before the Provisional Government's initiation of civil war:

> 'I fully agree with what you say about the neglect shown to our National Culture & those who have worked for it [...] I see that we must overthrow this civilization and this social system ... Let us draw the sword upon it and never cease from warfare till we have slain the Unclean Thing. We are strong enough & only we the Poets and Makers the worshippers of the Holy Earth which these things defile.'

The Wonder Smith, maker of worlds, analogises the struggle that Young describes to Campbell in epic heroic terms. Moreover, Young's privileging of the human element speaks especially to her new, American, audience that was in the pre-Crash thrall of consumer capitalism—a culture that Young would flee not long after her arrival in New York for the freedom and relative wilderness of California.

Lauren Arrington is Chair in Modern Literature at the Institute of Irish Studies, University of Liverpool; her most recent book is Revolutionary lives: Constance and Casimir Markievicz *(Princeton, 2016).*

Further reading

A. Annat, '"The Red Sunrise": gender, violence, and nation in Ella Young's vision of a new Ireland', in A. Pilz & W. Standlee (eds), *Advancing the cause of liberty: Irish women's writing 1878–1922* (Manchester, 2016).

R. Murphy, *Ella Young: Irish mystic and rebel* (Dublin, 2008).

E. Young, *Flowering dusk* (New York, 1945).

REVOLUTION SONG: IRISH NATIONALISTS AND GLOBAL MUSIC

BY **RICHARD PARFITT**

What should Ireland sound like? This was a question that troubled generations of Irish nationalists. For many, establishing Ireland as a nation was never solely or predominantly about independent political institutions.

Rather, activists expended a great deal of thought and energy in ensuring that Ireland existed as a culture distinct from its large and influential neighbour. We are most familiar with cultural revivalism in terms of the Irish language revival and the movement to create an Irish theatre. Music, however, was equally important to the history of Irish cultural nationalism.

Ireland's revolutionary generation was able to draw on several historical precedents. In 1792 the Belfast Harpers Assembly sought to revive a lost 'ancient' Irish harp culture. Meanwhile, political movements, including the United Irishmen (from whose number came the revolutionaries of 1798) and the Young Ireland writers of the 1840s, published songs celebrating 'liberty' and 'freedom' for Ireland inspired by the French Revolution. Their songs predicted a decisive French intervention in Ireland and pointed out that defeats had forced Britain to 'truckle to France', America and Russia.

In much the same way as the political ideology championed by nationalists, advocates of an authentically Irish music tradition expressed a belief in Ireland's ancient cultural distinctiveness whilst using language and symbols drawn from international comparisons and events. Revolutionary Ireland would draw on similar sources and ideas.

Irish music was an important concern for the Gaelic League. Although the League was founded in 1893 primarily to promote the Irish language, it often dedicated space in its newspaper, *An Claidheamh Soluis*, to music. The newspaper printed songs in Irish, advertised musical performances at Gaelic League festivals (*féiseanna*) and published articles by authors setting out their vision of how Irish music should sound.

Their efforts were undoubtedly

●

Left: Dubliner Peadar Kearney was the composer of numerous 'rebel' songs, including 'Down by the Glenside', 'The Tri-Coloured Ribbon' and 'The Soldier's Song', which was first published in 1912. (NMI)

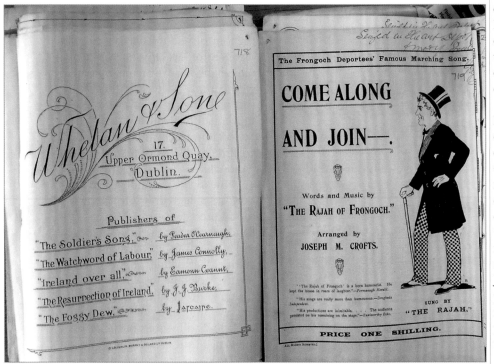

part of a global cultural phe-nomenon. Revivalists in nations such as Scotland, England, Germany and Hungary sought to identify their unique national music. These efforts focused on the musical cultures of the native rural peasantry, but were invariably influenced by an international and mobile intellectual élite. English folk-music revival-ist Cecil Sharp was a Cambridge-educated conductor who lectured at music colleges in Australia. In Ireland Dr Annie Patterson, the first woman in Britain or Ireland to hold a doctorate in music, was among the founders of the *Féis Ceoil* (Festival of Music). London provided one of the more important cosmopolitan centres in which these intellectuals

exchanged ideas. Indeed, it was the London Gaelic League, inspired by contact with Scottish revivalists, that introduced *céilidhe* (social evenings incorporating music and dance) to the organisation.

The *céilidh* was indicative of how international cultures influ-enced Ireland's revival. Like similar organisations across Europe, the Gaelic League located authentic national music in the folk cultures of the peasantry. They also followed equivalents abroad in identifying a 'gapped' scale, consisting of fewer notes than the conventional seven, as the musical basis of that culture. Just like their international counter-parts, Irish revivalists identified instruments that were considered part of the Irish sound. These included the harp, pipes and fiddle.

As part of the Restoration of Order in Ireland regulations passed in November 1920, the government interned suspected rebels in prisons and camps such as that at Ballykinlar in County Down. Although some of those interned reported that the prison authorities forced them to sing 'God Save the King' or deliberately restricted opportunities for musical recreation, nationalist prisoners during the Anglo-Irish War were mostly given free rein when it came to music. It raised the morale of the prisoners but ultimately did not undermine the purpose of the prison, which was to stop inmates from engaging in more practical acts of rebellion.

The revolutionaries who fought against British rule between 1919 and 1921 were heavily engaged in the musical cultures of the Gaelic

●
Above left: 'Come along and join'—republi-can songwriter Jimmy Mulkerns was better known as 'the Rajah of Frongoch' for his extravagant costumes and performances while interned in the Welsh camp after the Easter Rising.

●
Left: The 'Ballykinlar Players', put together by Mulkerns to entertain other internees in the County Down camp.

●
Opposite page: *Dora*, 'A Love Ditty on True Blue West British Lines', by Peadar Kearney, lampoons the Defence of the Realm Act, a key element in British wartime coercion.

Revival. In the internment camps, singing formed part of Irish-language classes run by the prisoners. A group of prisoners in Ballykinlar formed a fiddle band, consistent with the authentic Irish sound promoted by the Gaelic League. They played concerts for the other prisoners that included 'selections of Irish music' and provided the music for a *céilidh* to mark Labour Day in 1921.

Although Irish music and Irish songs were dwarfed by performances in English among the prisoners (songs including 'The West's Awake' and 'The Soldier's Song', written in English, were common), it is nevertheless significant that the prisoners chose to make unabashedly Irish music a part of their morale-boosting cultures during their imprisonment. 'Although we were debarred from working physically for our native land', reflected the Ballykinlar prisoners' newspaper *The Barbed Wire*, 'we have yet the opportunity for training our minds to work for the Better Ireland that is to be.'

The 'revival' of native music came to Ireland via transnational intellectual and cultural networks. At the same time, however, the revival was actively positioning itself against transnational musical cultures. The arrival of jazz in Ireland provides an illustrative example. Unlike most of the music that audiences were used to, jazz featured syncopated rhythms and was accompanied by dancing characterised by suggestive hip and arm movements. Jazz began in African-American communities in the United States before being introduced to France by US soldiers during the First World War. When Irish soldiers serving in the British army returned home, some brought an enthusiasm for this new genre with them. It was these former soldiers who established the first jazz clubs in Ireland in 1918 and 1919.

Some vocal advocates of Irish music responded with hostility and racism. When a judge in Clonmel considered whether to permit the opening of a new dancehall for jazz in November 1919, opponents argued that jazz came from Africa to America via 'a nigger who was afterwards lynched'. The music, they said, encouraged 'contortions of the body' and 'grimaces of a nigger' on the part of those dancing. They saw traditional music, in contrast, as a bulwark against 'vulgar' and 'trashy' cultures imported from abroad.

Even more controversial within the Gaelic movement was the tradition of music-hall. Jazz was a new arrival, but music-hall had been part of the Irish soundscape since the nineteenth century. Cultural nationalists regularly derided its lurid themes (tales of adultery and drunkenness were common) and English origins. Noting the 'less congenial atmosphere of the Anglicised music halls' in 1916, *An Claideamh Soluis* declared that, if Gaelic League branches maintained their commitment to Irish music, 'the problem of the music hall, cinema and ballroom is easily solved'. Recalling his

time in the revolutionary movement, former IRA member Seán Prendergast stated that 'music hall songs or those which might, even in the slightest way, be termed English were taboo'. This points to the desire of IRA members to ensure that their military aims appeared consistent with the aims of the Gaelic movement, but his comment is ultimately misleading.

In practice, music-hall formed a popular part of the Irish nationalist soundscape. Music-hall performances emphasised elaborate costumes, audience participation and characterful musical accompani-

●
Above: Countess Markievicz with members of Na Fianna band. The Fianna organised *céilidhe* and *féiseanna* for music, dance and drama. (NLI)

●
Opposite page: IRB leader Tom Clarke with the Laurence O'Toole Pipers' Band. Founded in 1910, the band was associated in its early years with both the republican and labour movements. (NLI)

ments (discordant harmonies accompanied lyrics about villains, while uplifting and rousing motifs were identified with references to heroes). These were also common features of Irish rebel songs. In the chorus of 'Memory of the Dead' (also known as 'Who Fears to Speak of '98?'), for example, a pause before the refrain, 'a true man, like you man, will fill your glass with us', encourages the audience to join in. At the same time, the full and rising accompaniment provides a typically rousing music-hall conclusion.

The republican songwriter Jimmy Mulkerns was one of several figures in the revolutionary movement who harnessed music-hall culture. Mulkerns was better known as the Rajah of Frongoch for his extravagant costumes and performances in the Frongoch internment camp after the Easter Rising. His songs were deliberately comic. In 'Come Along and Join the British Army', his best-known song, he

satirised the Irish Parliamentary Party's support for Britain's war effort by depicting its prominent MP Joseph Devlin as a recruiting agent:

Last week I met Joe Devlin,
And he took me by the hand.
Said he, your king and country need you,
Against the foe you ought to stand.
But I said I do not mind the Kaiser.
For that, said Joe, I'll make you very hot.
Because according to the law that is high treason.
So at dawn to-morro' morn I'll have you shot.

Devlin's name was sung to a discordant accompaniment, underlining his caricatured, villainous role. Devlin was a nationalist Home Ruler. In this portrayal, however, Devlin's loyalties were clearly not to Ireland but to an English king and his war on the German Kaiser. The song conveys the satirical mock-heroism of Devlin's offer by the farcically uplifting music that accompanies the line 'to-morro' morn I'll have you shot'. An image of Mulkerns wearing top hat, long coat and chequered trousers appears alongside the song in print. In both musical style and appearance, therefore, Mulkerns was a music-hall comic.

The government interned Mulkerns and other republican songwriters during the Irish Revolution. In Ballykinlar the music-hall songs and performances continued. Mulkerns formed the 'Ballykinlar Players', who put on comic performances for other internees (they heartily encouraged applications from those interested in playing fairies in a Christmas pantomime). Parodying their desire to be released, the prisoners held their 'First Farewell Concert' in 1921. Meanwhile, the humorous song 'The Mountjoy Boarding House', which described Dublin's Mountjoy Jail, where many republicans were imprisoned, was heavily reminiscent of music-hall. According to the song, Dublin boasted numerous houses 'with greatest propriety' but none compared to Mountjoy, where the 'waiters were trained with greatest ability' and served 'lamb and chicken with parsley cream'. Humour distracted from and belittled their incarceration. Music-hall, a genre imported from England and synonymous with English popular culture (or even Anglicisation), was not stamped out: rather, it was intrinsic to the national movement.

As well as drawing on transnational musical cultures, nationalist revolutionaries sought to prove that Ireland met international standards of nationhood. In the militaristic nationalist context of the early twentieth century, this came in the form of romantic patriotism and noble service to the nation. The sense of duty that inspired volunteers to join armies across Europe, as military historian Michael Howard has argued, reflected a Darwinian belief that the willingness and ability of men to fight and die for their country was proof of the nation's fitness to survive 'in a world where progress was the result, or so they believed, of competition rather than cooperation, between nations'.

This same transnational spirit of national duty inspired others to join the Irish Volunteers and later the IRA. The nationalists who fought against Britain for Ireland did not see themselves as subversives but rather as soldiers, legitimately representing the Irish nation in the same manner as soldiers fighting on the Continent represented their own countries.

The movement's defining anthem reflected this belief that the revolution represented a battle between the soldiers of two nations. 'Soldiers are we, whose lives are pledged to Ireland', the opening line of the chorus of 'The Soldier's Song', was more than a call to arms. It was also an assertion that a preparedness to die for the cause proved Ireland's nationhood. It is no coincidence that this song and its assertion of Ireland's nationhood became the anthem of the movement and the nation-state that it established. 'Kevin Barry', the ballad about a teenage IRA member executed for his part in killing a police officer, similarly depicted the titular character declaring 'Shoot me like a soldier / For I fought for Ireland'. His willingness to die made him a soldier: that he was a soldier made Ireland a nation.

The music of Ireland's revolution was at once national and transnational. Cultural and political activists in Ireland harnessed musical ideas and political ideals that crossed borders, expressing the distinctiveness and legitimacy of Irish culture in terms that reflected internationally framed understandings of nationalism and the nation. In their propaganda and cultural activism before and during the War of Independence, even in prison, the revolutionary generation drew on accessible, popular and international musical cultures that represented Ireland as an ancient culture and a legitimate nation.

Richard Parfitt is a historian based at the University of Oxford, specialising in Irish music and politics in the nineteenth and twentieth centuries.

Further reading

M. Gelbart, *The invention of folk music and art music* (Cambridge, 2007).

T. Moylan (ed.), *The indignant muse: poetry and songs of the Irish Revolution 1887–1926* (Dublin, 2016).

G.-D. Zimmermann, *Songs of Irish rebellion: political street ballads and rebel songs, 1780–1900* (Dublin, 1967).

'The Irish fight for liberty is the Greatest Epic of Modern History. It is a struggle that should have the sympathy and active support of every lover of liberty—of every member of an oppressed group. The Negro in particular should be interested in the Irish struggle, for while it is patent that Ireland can never escape from the menace of "the overshadowing empire" so long as England is able to maintain her grip on the riches and man-power of India and Africa it is also clear that those suffering together under the heel of British imperial-ism must learn to CO-ORDINATE THEIR EFFORTS before they can HOPE TO BE FREE ... The mighty tyrant is not to be toppled over by an unaided Ireland, however courageously her valiant sons may fight; nor yet by an Africa or India unaided ... until England is brought to the end of her rope there will be no freedom for Ireland, India or Africa.'

—Cyril Briggs, *The Crusader*, February 1921

Cyril Briggs, the West Indian leader of the left-wing African Blood Brotherhood, was one of several Caribbean radicals to identify with what he called 'Heroic Ireland's' rev-olution. Hubert Harrison from St Croix, 'the father of Harlem radical-ism', also urged his supporters to 'learn from Sinn Féin'. The most important black nationalist leader of the era, Jamaican-born Marcus Garvey, saw Ireland's cause as key to self-determination for all oppressed nationalities. Presiding over a mass rally of his Universal Negro Improvement Association in New York during August 1920, Garvey sent a message to de Valera asserting that 'We believe Ireland should be free even as Africa shall be free for the Negroes of the World. Keep up the fight for a free Ireland.' Garvey's influence was key when a few weeks later Irish longshoremen in New York boycotted British shipping in solidarity with Terence MacSwiney's hunger strike. Garvey facilitated meetings at his Harlem HQ, 'Liberty Hall', between African American and Irish dockworkers, which, despite a long history of antagonism between the two groups, led to black long-shoremen supporting the strike. In response, *The Messenger*, edited by socialist A. Philip Randolph, hoped that in future 'Negroes will be having their own Irish brothers strike for Negro freedom'. But while African American activists such as Randolph and W.E.B. Du Bois were sympathetic to the Irish cause, they were less effusive than the Caribbean natives Garvey and Briggs. This reflected the reality of racial conflict in the United States, where, as Du Bois put it, 'Irishmen (are) the race which Negroes as a whole dislike most'. During 1919 vicious race riots had exploded across America, and in cities such as Chicago Irish Americans were to the fore in deadly clashes with blacks. Nevertheless, Du Bois asserted that he would 'at all times defend the right of Ireland to absolute inde-pendence'. The issue was complicated by the rhetoric of some republican leaders when they toured America. De Valera, Harry Boland and Mary MacSwiney all on occasion declared that Ireland deserved freedom because it was 'the one remaining white nation in the slavery of alien rule'. They remained remarkably silent about the racial conflict taking place during their visits.

For many black activists, however, especially those born under British rule, it was not what the Irish thought about them but what Irish freedom might inspire among others that was important. Hence Garvey celebrated the Anglo-Irish Treaty as showing that 'the Irish have suc-ceeded, first among the trio of Egypt, India and Ireland, in winning a place of mastery among the nations of the world ... elevating Ireland and the Irish people from the position of serfs, peons, to that of masters'. And, as Briggs had asserted in *The Crusader*, 'the Irish people and the Negro people have much in common ... they are both oppressed by stronger groups. Secondly, the oppressors, in the main, of both Celt and Negro, are identified with the Anglo-Saxon race. Thirdly, the great enemy of the Irish people is also the greatest enemy of the Negro people. Not only does Great Britain tyrannize it over more Negroes and other colored races than are ruled by any other nation in the world, but Great Britain is also the bulwark of the Anglo-Saxon White Guards and of all the reactionary things for which they stand.'

The Irish struggle for independ-ence was led by men and women with very diverse views on racial questions, but their revolution itself was inspirational for many peoples seeking freedom from oppression.

●

Left: Marcus Garvey's newspaper, *Negro World*, announces a mass rally in New York for August 1920. This event sent greetings to de Valera and implored him to 'keep up the fight for a free Ireland'. (*Negro World*, 31 July 1920)